INDIA

INDIA:

THE LAND AND THE PEOPLE

SIR JAMES CAIRD, K. C. B. F. R. S.

GYAN

Published by

Gyan Publishing House
5, Ansari Road
Daryaganj, New Delhi-110002
Phone: 011-47034999, 9811692060
E-mail: books@gyanbooks.com

Distribution Network
gyanbooks.com
India, USA, Canada, UK, Australia, France

ISBN: 978-81-212-8818-7 (PB)
First Published, 1883

2nd Impression 2023

Printed at: Gyan Press, Delhi.

INDIA
Author: James Caird

INDIA
1879
Scale of English Miles
T I B E T
BAY OF BENGAL
ARABIAN SEA
BOMBAY
CALCUTTA
MADRAS
HAIDARABAD
CENTRAL PROVINCES
RAJPUTANA
Coromandel Coast
Malabar Coast
Laccadive Islands
Andaman Islands
Nicobar Is.
Ten Degree Channel
BURMAH
SIAM
MANDELAY
RANGOON
70 Long E. Gr.
75
80
85
90
95
10
15
20

INDIA:

THE LAND AND THE PEOPLE.

BY

SIR JAMES CAIRD, K.C.B., F.R.S.

WITH MAP OF INDIA.

CASSELL & COMPANY, LIMITED:

LONDON, PARIS & NEW YORK.

1883.

To

THE RIGHT HONOURABLE SIR LOUIS MALLET,

Late UNDER SECRETARY OF STATE FOR INDIA.

MY DEAR MALLET,

With your permission I dedicate to you this book on India and its People, with a warm acknowledgment of the valuable assistance you have readily afforded me in the consideration of questions which for the last twelve years have engaged your constant attention.

Believe me,

Sincerely yours,

JAMES CAIRD.

3, ST. JAMES' SQUARE,

Oct. 1883

PREFACE.

AFTER the great famine in India of 1876–7, the author was invited by the Marquis of Salisbury, then Secretary of State for India, to become a member of the Famine Commission, which was appointed by Her Majesty's Government to inquire into the whole circumstances of that calamity, with a view to the adoption of such means as might enable timely provision to be made to meet the inevitable recurrence, in that country, of seasons of dearth. The inquiry embraced the whole of India, and its results were embodied in the Report of the Commission, which has been laid before Parliament.

In traversing the country with the Members of the Commission, men eminent in their respective provinces, and two of them native gentlemen holding high office under native Princes, an unusually favourable opportunity for observation of the Land and the People was afforded. Whatever, at the time, appeared worthy of note was recorded in the author's note-book. And much was seen by a fresh eye, accustomed to seek reasons for diversity of systems affecting the prosperity of those engaged in the cultivation of the land, which is the chief business of the population of India.

The author desires to take the reader with him over the same course, from the outset of his journey at Southampton to his arrival in India, and thence over its various provinces, and on his return, through Egypt, to England. In the final chapters some special features of the policy which should be kept in view in our dealings with India are set forth, and certain main principles also which the author recommended in regard to the treatment of famine, on which the Commission were not fully agreed.

A portion of the narrative appeared in the pages of *The Nineteenth Century* on the author's return from India in 1879.

CONTENTS.

CHAPTER VIII.

MADRAS.

CHAPTER IX.

OOTACAMUND.—THE WYNAAD.—MYSORE.

CHAPTER XII.

EGYPT.

CHAPTER XIII.

INDIAN FAMINES AND THEIR LESSONS.

CHAPTER XIV.

THE FUTURE. CONCLUSION.

APPENDIX.

INDIA:

THE LAND AND THE PEOPLE.

CHAPTER I.

THE VOYAGE OUT.

On the 10th of October, 1878, I embarked at Southampton on the steamship *Bokhara* for Bombay. We had a severe gale going down channel. By the afternoon of the 11th we entered the Bay of Biscay, the ship rolling heavily though the wind had ceased. Next day there was a fine easterly breeze, the ship carrying all sail, with a smooth sea in the middle of the famous Bay. We passed Finisterre on Sunday morning, with a full cabin at the morning service, and were off Oporto as the sun went down, followed by a most lovely night, the full moon shining over the great expanse of calm but sparkling sea.

The morning of the 14th opened with lovely weather, the ships in sight all converging to the same point or coming from it—the entrance to the Straits. We pass a long range of coast, with Cape St. Vincent at the end of it, and in the background the last of a mountain range, culminating in Monchique, 3,000 feet high. The cape is a bleak spot—not a tree or shrub

B

to be seen on the long promontory where the lighthouse fronts the Atlantic, at a height of 100 feet on a solid rocky precipice, outside of which is a tall, pointed rock. Passing another bay the land recedes, and we stretch across the open sea towards Cape Trafalgar, where the "foremost sailor since the world began" fought his last great sea-fight.

Early on the 15th we were running into the anchorage at Gibraltar. The bareness and barrenness of the rock surprised me. It is literally a rock, with here and there scattered bits of brown vegetation, and, near the bottom, with clumps of acacia. The houses stretch behind the fortifications on the shore, where the water looks deep all along. Every shelving opening is faced with a crenellated wall. Landing from the ship your boat is rowed toward the walls, shoots round a corner, and lands you in a quiet little bay inside. Cabs are on the quay, which whisk over drawbridges and through openings in the walls, and then you are in the town. At every corner the red coat appears, and the streets have all English names—King Street, Queen Victoria Street, Church Street. Mules and the donkey are the beasts of burden. You buy nice sweet grapes in the market, 4 lbs. for sixpence. The chief articles are potatoes, sweet potatoes, onions, pomegranates, water-melons, and poultry. The country people look poor. The Governor with his aide-de-camp are going their morning round, 7 a.m., the guard turning out at each post. We were too early for the galleries of the fortressed rock, which are not shown before nine. But we saw the embrasures, along the mountain face, at great heights, through which the guns are pointed.

There is a neutral flat of ground of considerable space between the English and Spanish lines, beyond the latter of which, and within reach of modern artillery, is another rock on the Spanish side, nearly as high and large as Gibraltar itself. On this side the fortress is thought to be not impregnable to modern science and artillery. We drove to the back of the rock on the Mediterranean Sea, where the rock becomes a sheer precipice from near its summit, 900 feet high.

On the African side of the Straits rises a similar rocky promontory—Ceuta. The Straits are thus naturally provided with a fitting gateway from the ocean to the great inland sea, through which, inwards and outwards, is passing the traffic of widely-severed lands. The Bay itself includes the Spanish town of Algesiras, sparkling white in the sunshine, a gay contrast with the more sober hue of the brown Gibraltar. We leave it rapidly behind as we speed out into the Mediterranean, with a strong wind carrying us along. During the night there was heavy rain, with thunder and lightning, which cleared the air, ushering in with brightness the new morning. The wind has fallen and the air is warm.

The arrangements for the comfort of the passengers on board are excellent. There are about 100 first class, and 50 second class, and as many children of both classes. Tea is to be had at six in the morning, breakfast at nine, luncheon one, dinner six, and tea at half-past eight. The cookery is good, and all served hot and plentiful. The cook's place, in which all is done, is not the fourth size of an ordinary kitchen. Everybody is well served, and the waiting at table is good—a steward to every six persons. The air is so warm (October 19th) that, though the wind is blowing half a gale, all the ventilators are open, and sitting in your chair on deck the breeze fans you, and the draught never seems to injure you. There are awnings all along the deck, and an apron put below them on the sunny side to more effectually keep out the sun.

Algeria is on our right, and we sail along its coast the whole day and night, passing Galita early in the morning, and Zembra, an island at the mouth of the Bay of Tunis. A high mountainous range is seen in the background behind the cultivated coast-line. We round the northernmost point of Africa, and next morning are at anchor in the harbour of Malta, after going slowly along a yellow rocky shore, through a lovely clear calm sea.

The wider view of the city from the deck is very picturesque. It is a mass of fortifications, with an outer and inner harbour, behind which the town rises to some height. At the highest point are the quarters of the artillery, where we were hospitably invited to breakfast. It is the old Auberge de Castile, the former palace of the Knights of Spain in Malta, and very spacious and splendid. The streets are very picturesque, though narrow and steep. The houses are solid and large, and all with pretty varieties of covered balconies on the different storeys. The palace, now the residence of the Governor, was the ancient palace of the Grand Master of the Knights of Malta, whose throne-room is still extant. It is in the centre of the city, the place in front of it adorned with oleander trees, now covered with their pretty pink flowers.

Near it is the great church, the gem of Malta. It is quite beautiful—one grand hall; no pillar to interrupt the sight or sound. At the altar end it is magnificent—beautiful sculpture, beautiful colour, marble, gold, lapis lazuli, grand roof, and all along the two sides of the hall a special chapel for each country which sent forth Crusaders. Each chapel seems more lovely than the other, with Raffaels, Domenichinos, sculpture, gold, and precious stones: not railed off from the grand central hall, but yet each, in its recess, distinct. The whole floor of the hall is paved with marble slabs, on each a shield with the name and title of the Knights, several of whom are English—Earl Beauchamp, Merivale, and others. The whole is kept in the most excellent order, the revenues of the Archbishop and church being large.

The rock of the island is a soft freestone, which is hewn almost as you could hew wood with an axe, when it comes fresh from the quarry. After exposure it becomes hard and tough. But the ease with which it can be wrought has enabled the people to build themselves grand and solid houses.

We had not time to visit the Bay where St. Paul landed from his shipwreck, which is five miles distant from the city. There can be no doubt, on tracing the voyage on the chart, that it was on this island the "barbarous" people received the Apostle and his companions so hospitably. Melita is still the name of the island. But the Roman Catholics, who have been so long dominant here, and who show such reverent care for their Cathedral, have raised no special memorial in the Bay.

Next day we were off the Lybian Desert, thermometer, 2 p.m., 76°. A lovely calm day, with just breeze enough to temper the great heat. We are now beginning to taste the climate of Asia, putting away the English and getting out the Asian clothes.

Next morning we are nearing Port Said. The sea has lost its rich blue colour, and has become light green, and less transparent. We have now passed the mouths of the Nile, and, though 80 miles from shore, the mud of the great river still tinges the sea. There is a piano on deck, on which the ladies in turn discourse sweet music. Every one is now at home on the sea, and the weather is so fine, and the sea so smooth, and the ship so easy, that all enjoy it.

In the morning of the 23rd of October we were off Port Said; thermometer, 7 a.m., 75°. I was called at five to see the first of the land of Egypt, and the entrance to the famous Suez Canal. The sun had not risen, but when he rose his splendour cleared all haze away. The lights on the lighthouse and light-ships were at once extinguished, and numerous steamers and vessels were descried, all converging on Port Saide. On the right a long breakwater stretches out, made of large blocks of concrete laid loosely in rows. The shore is sand, all is sand, low sandy coast. The first living creature to be seen was a dog, then another, exactly of the wolfish type one sees on the Egyptian marbles. Native boats, laden to the gunwale, stretch away seawards. We pass the lighthouse, then all kinds of temporary Eastern houses, and on the shore a crowd of bare-legged people with picturesque turbans on their heads. Porpoises play about the ship as we come in, and small birds of various foreign aspect light upon our decks. A large steamship of the Ducal line, which we overtook at Cape St. Vincent and passed, and which again passed us while lying at Gibraltar; again overtaken by us before we reached Malta, and passing us whilst there; again overtaken, and passed by us in the night, is now seen on the horizon following us in.

At 3.30 p.m., thermometer 81°, we are working through the Canal: a most difficult navigation in any part, but in the straight runs, there is so little room, and going at little over four miles an hour, not steerage-way for a long heavy ship. We were for a short time stuck fast. Part of the way the banks were rich alluvial soil, but, the climate being rainless, without vegetation. Nearing Ismailia we pass for miles along banks of barren sand, stretching away as far as the eye can reach. Here is a ferry across the Canal to serve the track from Jerusalem, which may have been trodden by Joseph when, with Mary and the infant Jesus, he fled to Egypt. Troops of loaded camels pass along the banks of the Canal, driven by picturesque Arabs. The lakes skirted by it are shallow, and immense flocks of flamingoes and pelicans, countless in number, stand fishing in the waters. The privilege to fish and take wild fowl in these lakes is let for £60,000 a year. A group of children follow the ship along the bank, to pick up apples or oranges thrown to them, clothed literally in nothing but their own dusky skin, clean-limbed and active. They are attended by a serious looking dog, which runs straight after them, taking no heed of anything but them. Once he seemed to find the steady pace too warm for him, and he hopped down the bank and ran along within the edge of the water for a while, and then jumped up and resumed his business-like attendance—a wolf-looking dog, but with evident sympathy for his dusky human friends. At Ismailia the fresh-water canal from the Nile, which supplies all the inhabited part of the desert with the only water it possesses, pours its superfluity into the great Canal.

The Suez Canal is, indeed, a work more wondrous than all the other wonders of Egypt. This grand waterway, which connects the vast commerce of the East and West, is now also a salt-water boundary between Asia and Africa. The anticipated difficulties of keeping it open have not been experienced. The sand does not blow in in any quantity which cannot be taken out with ease, and at little cost. And the generous character of the great engineer who constructed it is shown by his acknowledgment of the earlier efforts of the English Lieutenant Waghorn who established the overland route, by the statue of him erected by M. de Lesseps, in acknowledgment of these efforts, near the eastern end of the Canal. I recall the debate in the House of Commons on Mr. Roebuck's motion, 25 years ago, when only one-tenth of its members supported this scheme, which is already unparalleled in the beneficence and grandeur of its results. It was vigorously opposed by Lord Palmerston and Mr. Disraeli, and declared to be physically impracticable by Robert Stephenson, the engineer. But it was supported with clearer prescience by Mr. Gladstone, Lord John Russell, Mr. Bright, Mr. Roebuck, and Mr. Milner Gibson. Among the more distinguished of its supporters who have now passed away were Sir James Graham, Sidney Herbert, W. J. Fox, Sir Charles Napier, W. S. Lindsay, and General Thompson. Among those who voted for it, and are still with us, were Mr. Hastings Russell, now Duke of Bedford, Mr. W. E. Baxter, Mr. Ayrton, Sir Robert Collier, Mr. Dilwyn, Mr. Kinglake, Lord Arthur Russell, Sir John Trelawny, and myself. The only member of the present Government who voted on either side was Mr. Gladstone. These were the "waifs and strays, not then looked upon as good company in any assembly of politicians," quaintly referred to by him in the recent debate on the Suez Canal.

Entering the Red Sea, which we did at the full height of the sun, the effect of colour was singularly beautiful. The sea itself in the Gulf of Suez under this light is bright green. The Bay, forming the wide arc of a circle, is edged by a broad border of bright yellow sand, and thence to the summit of the mountain range, nearly 4,000 feet high, the colour is the hue of red. The effect of the green, yellow, and red in the sunshine, on so grand a scale, is wonderfully fine.

Oct. 25th, 9.30. p.m., therm. 78°, Red Sea. The junction here with the passengers from Brindisi has nearly doubled our numbers. A bishop, a judge, and other considerable people have joined. A fine breeze blows behind us all day, but not oppressively hot, not more so than a very warm sunny summer day at home. Except for the barren deserts of sand, the outline is not unlike Loch Lomond at its widest part, but the serrated ridges of mountain behind are absolutely bare—no grass, bush, or vegetation, nor sign of fresh water, or human habitation.

From the judge of the High Court at Calcutta, to which all appeals finally come, I learn that nine-tenths of the litigated cases in India are decided by native judges, who hold the courts of first instance, in all cases not of a criminal kind. The native judge is said to be in some cases timid, and afraid of criticism, and apt, if called to account, though in the right, to offer excuses with too little regard to the facts. Such men require to be steadied by association with a British judge.

An Indigo planter on board tells me that his father, forty years ago, took up a grant of 60,000 acres of land on the borders of Nepaul. The land has now been cleared, and is let to natives, who, besides their food, grow indigo for him. He makes advances to them, and takes the crop at a price according to quality, and prepares it for export, with a good profit. He likes the people, but says they are improvident, and that nothing will teach them care or saving. They live for the day, and think of nothing beyond it. There is a German missionary on his estate who is an excellent man, but he was no success except with the young in schools. The Zenana Mission is conducted by the missionary's wife, and with more success, as the native women, even of the higher class, are very ignorant, and can only be reached by female teachers.

On the deck, under the awning, as the ship speeds on her way, much may be learned from the conversation of men of experience on board. Here is an opium and indigo civilian officer, who has been nine years among the cultivators, and likes and pities them. They are so poor that they dare not resent oppression, and there is no public opinion on their side. In Behar, in this officer's district, there are 60,000 acres of indigo and 45,000 of poppy, the cultivation of both being carried on by the ryots under advances; the first from the planters, the second from the Government.

The best land is used for the poppy, and the second quality for the indigo: the poppy gives much the best return to the cultivator at the price paid to him by the Government, who, in their turn, sell it by auction at Calcutta, with an enormous profit.

An irrigation officer describes the country in which his work has lain. Water can always be found in Behar within thirty feet of the surface, and wells that depth, of dry masonry, cost £9, inclusive of material and labour. A well suffices for five acres of land, and a family with a well, and that extent of land, can protect themselves against famine. Not more than one-third of the holding should be irrigated each year, especially if from canals, so as not to exhaust the land; for the ryot cannot find manure for more than one-third, and the water is always most profitable when applied to the manured land. The indigo cultivation, if unmanured, rapidly exhausts the land. Wheat, at the present cost of carrying from the interior, cannot he thinks be profitably exported to England when the price there is not more than forty shillings a quarter. But there is great scope in Assam and Burmah for the extension of business of all kinds. No one has yet been able to devise a method for the release of the poor cultivator from the domination of the native banker.

Sunday evening, 27th Oct., off Mount Elba (7,000 feet), Nubia, 10 p.m., thermometer 90°. This is the hottest day we have had, with very little wind. Away in the west there is a sudden great flush in the sky, answered by another some miles farther north. This has been going on at regular short intervals for the last two hours. There is no thunder audible. The sea is smooth; the sky cloudy and without stars. The punka is kept constantly going during meals; and very refreshing are the raspberry ices at lunch. The next two days are still hotter. In the early morning we pass a tall rocky islet; in the forenoon the Twelve Apostles, a cluster of picturesque volcanic islands. At 8 p.m. we sight Mocha, famous for its coffee, pass Perim at midnight, and expect to be at Aden in the morning.

When the ship dropped anchor we were at once surrounded by native boys from Aden, in canoes, from which they dive with wonderful quickness for coin thrown over into the sea for them. They are lively black shiny fellows, whom the sharks won't touch. Aden is a volcanic peninsula, joined by a low strip of sand to the mainland of Arabia. It rises in a succession of hills to a peak at least 1,000 feet high. There is a fine deep harbour, with depôts of coal on the quays, and supplies for the British navy. Rain seldom falls here, and there is not a spring of water. But there are great tanks, cut in the solid rock, to store the rain when it does fall. The main supply, however, is got by condensing the sea-water, which, when deprived of its salt, is wholesome. Aden is an outpost of India, a strong place, garrisoned by artillery and troops, the gate of the Red Sea thus kept safe for England.

We landed in the Governor's boat, in a bay below his house. The sand, as I leapt ashore, felt like a hot furnace. But, on ascending the rocky hill on which the Residency is placed, the air in the breeze was more cool, and life more endurable. A verandah surrounds the house, which is a series of lofty open apartments, one after the other, kept cool by a lattice-work of "tatties" on the outside. Here, on a barren rock, projecting into the sea from a long spit of land in Arabia, without a particle of verdure, must the watchman of the gateway dwell during his five years incumbency as its guardian. Our party was received with much kindness and hospitality by General Loch. There was the luxury of ice in plenty, and very delicious; and we were waited on by natives in the most noiseless and attentive manner.

The same evening we were steaming out to the Indian Ocean, the moon shining from a starlit sky on a sparkling line of foam straight behind us, a German gentleman singing his spirited Rhine song with a fine voice on the quarter-deck. In the hot weather many of the passengers sleep on deck. Next morning the captain was exercising his men at the boats, and then had the fire-alarm bell rung, every man running to his quarters.

November 3rd the ship is stopped. Some bearings have become overheated, and as there is time to spare we stop to let them cool. The ship lies rolling in the swell without forward motion. Croakers are saying that something has gone seriously wrong with the engines, and as we have 800 miles still to go, and a head wind, they reckon we may take a fortnight, may be a month, to do it. The water is deliciously clear and blue, and lo! a great shark swims slowly up, attended by a group of sparkling fish, like herrings in size, that always follow him. A line and hook is got ready, and, well baited, is dropped in front of him. The monster comes up, and, passing once or twice slowly round, he throws himself on his back, his white belly gleams, he has swallowed the bait, is hooked, and at our mercy! With a rush he throws himself wildly about. We dare not pull him up, as the hook has only caught through the gristle of his mouth. There is running to get a rope with a noose to slip down the line, and over his fins, and thus draw him up. But before that can be accomplished the ship heaves up with the swell, the line is drawn too tight, his whole weight is upon it, the hook cuts through the cartilage, and with a wild sweep he is gone! Meantime the bearings have cooled, the screw is at work again, and the ship goes on. In three days more we are nearing Bombay, and feel thankful to Captain Ormond and the officers and crew of the good ship *Bokhara*, who have brought us to the end of a fortunate voyage without a single mishap.

CHAPTER II.

BOMBAY TO CAWNPORE.

BOMBAY is the second city in the British Empire in population, 650,000, with an average to the square mile exceeding that of London. The average number of persons to each house in London is eight, and in Bombay twenty-one. Sixty-six per cent. are Hindus, 21 per cent. Mohammedans, the rest Parsees, Jews, native Christians, and Europeans. The average death-rate for five years was almost the same as that of London. The rateable value of the city has fallen within the last nine years nearly one-third. It is situated on an island with an area of twenty-two square miles, which is joined by a short embankment to the mainland, and draws its daily supplies partly from the island, but chiefly from the mainland, by market boats which crowd the bay, and ply along the neighbouring coasts and inland creeks.

Under the experienced guidance of the Commissioner of Police, I traversed the city, visiting the very extensive wet dock about to be opened, and the handsome city markets lately erected. Every sort of thing is there for sale—vegetables, fruit, flowers, corn, butter, meat, fish, salt, live poultry, parrots, and monkeys. Then passing along the streets we came, in the middle of the old city, to a sacred tank, about the size of a large square in London, full of water, not very clean, to which people run in from the streets and bathe, whilst others are washing clothes. On one side is a sacred temple, the roof covered with pigeons. There was an unsavoury odour from this sacred tank, which seems to be replenished by the rain as it runs off the houses and streets; but in this hot climate, where the people have little clothing and do not mind getting it wet, the water seemed a welcome refuge from the heat and dust to hundreds coming and going. The streets are most quaint and picturesque, every house having its own peculiar architecture and special decorative colouring. The shopkeepers are all seated cross-legged in their open shops, many taking coffee with their customers, and crowds of people are stalking along the streets. The syces with our carriage call out to clear the way, there being risk of knocking people down at every step. They are tall, thin, but stately people, varied and picturesque in their attire, contented-looking, and all seeming to have some object in view, most of them with fine intelligent eyes.

At a cotton-mill in the suburbs, which I visited, the native owner was anxious to deprecate any advantage of cheap labour being in his favour compared with our cotton-spinners at home. "It takes 1,200 people here to do what 500 can with you, and then they are so idle." He took us to see their houses—huts placed in flat ground under the shade of great trees. They are such as one would suppose would breed fever—but the people are said to be very healthy—wide, low houses, the roofs covered with broad leaves down to within two feet of the ground, no window, and a low door through which any grown person must almost creep. But the thickly-thatched roof and the absence of windows keep out the sun, and the people take their food generally out of doors. The little naked children looked quite healthy. In the mills the people seemed to carry on the work much as with us. The hours of work are from six to six, with an hour at midday for meals and rest. The monthly wages are for a girl or boy 10s., a woman 16s., and a man 32s. They have English machinery, with cheap labour, and native cotton, but coal 40s. a ton. The Indian cotton has 15 per cent. of size in it, the English much more, according to my Indian informant. Besides supplying the local demand there is an export of twist and yarn, valued at £400,000, which goes chiefly to China.

In the evening we walked on Malabar Hill, a picturesque promontory near the city, where the Governor and other high officials and merchants reside. We passed an extensive enclosed ground on the summit of the ridge, on which there is a tower, inhabited by vultures which are protected by the Parsees, who dispose of their dead there. Every day or two there is a funeral. The birds watch its approach from their "Tower of

Silence." The body is carried to an open chamber in the tower, and in about fifteen minutes every particle of flesh is cleared off the bones by the unclean birds, and the bones drop down into a dry well, where they remain for subsequent removal. On our return home in the lovely moonlight we passed the Hindu cemetery and saw a funeral pyre, on which the body of a deceased Hindu was, after their fashion, being burnt.

Next day we crossed the bay to the famous rock caves of Elephanta. There was a fine breeze, but the sun was broiling, even though we had a thick wooden awning on the steam launch. The bay is extremely beautiful and capacious, with islands and capes, wooded and precipitous, and a distant coast outline running to a height of 4,000 feet. As there have been heavy rains lately, the low islands are quite green, and most refreshing to the eye after the barren rocks and sandy deserts of the Red Sea.

The caves are about 250 feet above the level of the sea, and approached by a long series of steps, tolerably shaded by trees. The woods were vocal with the song of birds, and lizards ran along the walls with great speed. On the little flat pieces of land, formed by the careful labour of centuries, plots of rice were being harvested. Entering the caves, which, with the pillars and great figures, are all cut out of the solid rock, there is an air of wonderful majesty. The great figures, repeated again and again, are the Hindu Trinity—the Creator, the Preserver, and the Destroyer.

In Bombay I had an opportunity of hearing the views of experienced official men on many topics of interest. In regard to railways the facility of transport has increased prices, and especially those of articles of largest bulk. As wheat and other grain can be carried at a halfpenny a ton a mile, the food of the people in India will probably rise greatly in price to the benefit of the producers, but to the injury of the dwellers in towns and cities. These are now complaining of the rise in price as one result of British rule, and are discontented. As the price of food grain hitherto has been lower than in other countries the non-producer feels the increase of price severely. This is an experience precisely the opposite of ours, where home-produced corn was dearer than in other countries, and the facilities of transport have cheapened it in favour of the consumer, and against the interest of the producer.

As a test of the failure of food the records of the Bombay Mint, in the years of the last famine, are very instructive. The quantity of up-country silver, chiefly melted ornaments, transmitted to the Mint in part of the years 1876, 1877, and 1878, embracing 23 months, amounted to the value of nearly £2,000,000. The first occasion on record in which the people sold their ornaments for food, in sufficient quantities to cause the bullion to reach the Mint, was during the bad years of 1871-2. Previous to that no silver that had passed up-country ever found its way back to the Bombay Mint.

If the salt tax, which bears with most crushing weight on the poorest, as it is a necessary of life which must be consumed by him as freely as by the rich, could be dispensed with, great would be the gain to the mass of the population. The wealthy Zemindars, merchants, rich natives, and highly-paid officials are lightly taxed, and enjoy the protection of Government without paying adequately for it. The opposition to a policy in this direction is believed to have been much over-estimated, as it would really be confined to a comparatively small body of wealthy persons who would be the last to find any advantage in disturbing the security of British rule. An income tax on all persons with an income over 250 rupees would bring in a considerable revenue without undue pressure. A saving might at the same time be made by employing fewer Europeans, and those only in the highest departments, and by substituting natives in all posts for which they are capable, and at native rates of pay.

The change from payment of rent, or Government assessment, in kind, to payment in cash, is believed by many to have led directly to the almost universal dependence of cultivators on the money-lender. In the former plan, when a bad season came, the assessment declined, as it was a proportion of the crop. That proportion being much lower than is taken by native governments, the advantage of living under British rule could be clearly seen; and by payment in produce there would be no need of the costly system of re-assessment, as, if there was a general rise of price, the Government would obtain its fair share of that advantage on their proportion of the crop.

Leaving Bombay for the interior on the 8th of November, I travelled by the line of the Great Indian Peninsular Railway. The stations along the line are very neat, and covered with creepers and flowers, and with the plants one sees in the tropical department of the public gardens at home, with crimson and other richly-coloured leaves. Every village and station seems full of people. The railway runs up the bank of the Kalu for some miles. This is a broad tidal river, with many boats plying to and fro. Near its bank are numerous small rice-fields, the crop of which is now being reaped with the reaping-hook. Thermometer 84°, 10 a.m. Among the cultivated fields there is no lack of trees, which have an advantage over ours in always being green. They are the palm, pepul, bur, tamarind, and kyra, the last a low tree on which the camels browse. They are dotted over the landscape, and afford a certain amount of shade, and generally near villages there is a grove of trees.

Every now and then we pass a group or village of huts, very poor mud fabrics, covered with fibrous plants and leaves. Patches of good land, where water can be applied, are all that is here cultivated. Outside the villages, and shaded by the trees, there is generally a wide ditch, full of very dirty water, in which one may, during the heat of the day, by careful looking discover the village kine, the water buffalo, black creatures with no hair, and long twisted horns turned backwards, lying in the mud, for coolness. Pack bullocks, laden with grain, pass along the road, straying into the stubbles to pick up anything that may have been left. The background of mountains begins to shut us in, and after four or five hours in the flat country we commence our ascent of the Western Ghats. This is the range of mountains which, arresting the rains of the south-west monsoon, feeds the great rivers that water the peninsula from Poonah to Cape Comorin.

After climbing 1,800 feet, by my barometer, through a pretty, wooded, hilly country with steep gradients, we reach the summit station, where I entered into conversation with a stout English employé on the line, who said it was an enormous business to work the trains "up these 10,000 feet." "Nonsense," I said, "it is not 2,000." "Ah!" said he, "a stranger might think so, but he knew every foot of it, having been at the making of the line." I did not insist, as he evidently gave no heed to the little tell-tale aneroid in my hand. He and his wife and children enjoyed good health. He gets his meat "tolerable," but "don't go in for curry and rice, and such like, as he sticks to English living—meat, vegetables, and pudding." They have three English clergymen and one Roman Catholic, and a good English school. The train moves on, I wishing him good fortune, and he for me a prosperous journey.

We soon arrive at Nasick, a very ancient city, through which the infant Godavery flows, and which is dammed up at three places for the daily baths of the citizens. This great river rises some fifty miles farther up, and, flowing through a sacred tank, issues thence by a golden spout, gathering volume as it goes from the monsoon rains, and, after a course of many hundred miles, discharges a portion of its waters through Sir Arthur Cotton's irrigation canals over the rich delta into the Bay of Bengal.

After passing the summit, the land does not fall to the level whence we rose on the west, but continues a lofty cultivated table-land at an altitude of 1,800 feet. The night felt cold, but the day was quite as warm as at Bombay, though not so close. The surface is undulating and fairly cultivated. Patches of wheat are just coming through the ground, and everywhere the people are busy sowing it. The plough is drawn by a pair of small buffalo bullocks, the ploughman being accompanied by a woman, with a basket of wheat, who trickles the seed in in front of the plough, in the bottom of the last furrow, in an excellent seed-bed, the plough at once closing in the ground over it, and effectually preserving it from birds. Less than one bushel of seed thus suffices, and it comes up thick enough. As many as ten ploughs follow each other, the village in this case appearing to do its work in common. The famine touched this part of the country, but not severely, as there are many people and cattle everywhere, and the land seems fully cultivated. The sheep and cattle, and tall goats, all graze together on the fallows and common pasture. Before dark we reach an elevation of 2,000 feet of this cultivated land; and in the morning, when daylight comes, I find that during the night we have descended 1,200 feet.

We are now in the valley of the Taptee River—very good land. This river is here about as large as the Thames at Windsor, and flows westward, past Surat, to the sea. The "valley" is really a plain about 600 feet above sea-level, covered with crops—bajri (great millet), and jowar (spiked millet), very much alike, with a stalk like Indian corn, the seed carried in a bunch at the top, the stalk from six to ten feet high, and very good fodder. Dhall is a plant growing in rows like small gooseberry-bushes with yellow flower and the seed a pea. Tobacco, sugar-cane, cotton (very small crop), are all nearly ripe. Wheat is being sown and coming up, and ripens in March. The people all seem busy early and late, and every one is out of doors, all very lightly clad. In the bajri crop, now ripening, there is a tripod set up with a stand higher than the top of the tall crop, on which a native is perched, who employs himself in shouting, and slinging stones, to frighten the birds.

We cross the ridge dividing the plain of the Nerbudda from that of the Taptee. Here the land is poor, and many hundreds of square miles are in jungle—the elevation about 2,000 feet. The small rivers are becoming dry, and many of them then serve for six months the very useful purpose of roads. The jungle is not unlike the barer parts of the New Forest, but there are no young plantations on it. For the next sixty miles the country is nearly all jungle, well watered by streams, and therefore a favourite resort of the tiger. He never shows above the tall grass. The cultivation occasionally passed is poor, and so are the villages. At Itarsi, as we descend, the land improves, is a deep, strong, yellow-brown loam, and is now mostly in wheat. The wheat seems to follow some other grain-crop, the stubble having been turned in some weeks back, and the seed-furrow and sowing is now being done. We were here in the valley of the Nerbudda, a large and productive wheat country. Thermometer 88° at 4 p.m., at 1,000 feet elevation.

During the second night we had descended from Jubbulpore—300 to 400 feet—and now, in this part of the Gangetic plain, are at 350 feet above the sea-level. The soil is a whitish, loamy marl, carefully tilled, but with very little help of manure. The usual crops are growing; wheat is being sown in small patches. The villages are mean and poor, and indicate great poverty. We cross the Jumna and enter Allahabad. It is often remarked that India has been denuded of trees. I can only say that, in the 900 miles I have traversed from Bombay, the country is quite as well clothed as most English counties. Then there are great breadths of wild wood-land—jungle—not good enough to be cultivated, and left in a state of nature. These afford cheap grazing for cattle, the trees not being close together, as in our woods, but with plenty of sun and air between them to admit of the growth of high thick grass, in which deer, and some tigers also, are found.

Allahabad lies in the fork formed by the junction of the Jumna with the Ganges, 500 miles north-west of Calcutta. It has a population of 143,000, and is the seat of the Government of the North-West Provinces. The fort, a place of strength both by nature and art, is on the edge of the Jumna, with one side commanding also the Ganges to the junction of the rivers. The country is a wide alluvial plain as far as the eye can reach. The Jumna at this season appears the largest river, the Ganges being low, with a great breadth of dry sand-banks. The native town is very mean, but full of people. Most of the houses have gardens, which yield their owners vegetables. The native houses are poor, with no sign of architecture or permanence. There are many ruins, but none that I saw of much importance. The new part of the town, where the English reside, is laid out with fine broad roads at right angles, bordered by trees giving ample shade. There is a museum, and gardens and public park, kept in beautiful order, regularly watered to keep it green. There are miles of these fine roads, all named after English officers of the civilian branch of the service. A handsome memorial church to Lord Mayo has just been completed. Near it splendid crops of bajri, ten feet high, are growing, on one head of which I reckoned 2,000 grains. The houses of the English, and the English shops, are all large villas in their own grounds, or "compounds."

One of the judges of the High Court called and spent the evening with me. He finds the people not more litigious than those of London. The Bunyia or native banker he considers a most useful class, who do not charge higher rates of interest, on the doubtful security they receive, than are common in London where bills of similar quality are renewed every three months, and charged five per cent. interest, and five per cent. commission. He expressed a strong objection, in which my subsequent inquiries led me entirely to concur, to the system of famine relief camps, and to placing the people on public works distant from their homes, preferring to relieve them as much as possible in their villages through the head men.

Next morning I left Allahabad for Cawnpore. The land is nearly flat all the way—120 miles—with just sufficient undulation to admit of drainage and irrigation. The millet is everywhere strong and tall. When cut, the stooks stand up ten feet high, and would astonish an English farmer. The castor-oil plant is extensively cultivated, and is a fine, noble plant, with large baylike leaves. It is grown chiefly for machine-oil for the railways. The wheat is coming up, and the great effort of the farmer is to give it, at this early stage, a cover of irrigation-water.

Much of this part of the country is poor, and shows signs of the rhé salt, which in certain localities comes up over the surface and renders it barren. The land is in some places covered with jungle, and is all more or less a whitish clay loam, becoming less cultivated where it is most stiff. It seemed to me that more fruit-trees might be planted with advantage. The mango and the orange thrive when properly managed. I have, for the first time, seen pigs here turned out in the fields to grub or graze. There is very little grass, barer than the barest Down on the driest summer day in England; but the half-starved, hungry cattle all do their best to find a living on it. How immensely would the power of keeping good stock be increased by irrigation, applied to forage-crops in this hot climate!

Cawnpore is a considerable place, with a population of 123,000, and has become a great changing mart to which the general produce of the country is sent, sold in the market, and distributed by railway to Calcutta or Bombay.

Here I visited the too famous "Well." The scene of the tragedy has been converted into a beautiful park, with walks and flowers, cypress and weeping willows, all kept in perpetual verdure by the most careful gardening and liberal supply of water. None but Europeans are permitted to enter freely. All natives, unless furnished with a pass, are excluded from the grounds, and altogether from the inclosure round the Well. The inscription is, "Sacred to the memory of a great company of Christian people, chiefly women and children, who near this spot were cruelly murdered by order of the Nana Dundapoot of Bithoor, and cast, the dying with the dead, into the well below." No games or amusements are allowed, and carriages must go at a foot pace. When I entered the inclosure I felt as one standing on holy ground. The figure of the angel by

Marochetti is very fine, the face expressing sorrow mingled with indignation. The structure inclosing the well was designed by Col. Yule, C.B. This is the scene of the cruel murder of the ladies and children in July, 1857, by the miscreant, Nana. I then visited the Memorial Church, which stands close to the intrenchment within which the gallant Sir Henry Wheeler defended himself and his small force till betrayed by the Nana's promise to let them escape by the river, in boats, if they would give up their position, which, for lack of ammunition, and in the burning sun of July, had become untenable. I walked from it down the lane to the Ghaut, on the Ganges, by which the doomed party were conducted to the boats in which they were treacherously fired at, and murdered, the women and children being brought back to the awful fate reserved for them. Cawnpore and its cruel massacre must ever have a thrilling interest in the memory of the English people.

I here met the other members of the Famine Commission, and in their company continued my observations while in India.

The agriculture of the neighbourhood is good. The land is owned by Zemindars, who cultivate part of it themselves, and let part to tenants. They grow carrots and potatoes for sale as garden crops, both of which are lightly manured and well watered by irrigation. Bajri is the principal food-corn, and pulse is grown with it to ripen as a second crop. A patch of the castor-oil plant is found on most farms, also wheat and barley, but no forage-crop. The land is clean, friable, moved to a depth of eight inches, below which the subsoil is permeable by air and moisture. I walked over the land of a village within five miles of Cawnpore, and found the crops all good, and the young wheat and barley coming up. These are watered from a main irrigation channel, provided by Government, from which the cultivator makes his own offset into a small pond, wide enough to contain such a head of water as admits of two water-baskets being worked by four men, with a lift of about eight feet, up which they throw the water into channels, which distribute it over the crops at the rate of one acre a day. This they arrange and maintain at their own cost. The water was being turned upon the growing wheat, patch after patch, in a most skilful and careful manner. The four men are relieved by four others by turns, so as to maintain an uninterrupted flow from morning to night. The hired men each receive threepence a day and half a pound of parched grain. The produce of wheat is about sixteen bushels an acre, little more than half of an English crop. On such land, with water, light, and heat in abundance, the crop might be doubled by an application of nitrate of soda, but at the respective values here of wheat and nitrate there would be little profit. Nitrate of soda pays on suitable land with wheat at 6s. a bushel, but would leave no profit on wheat at 3s. It was selling in the market in November, 1878, at the unusually high rate of 4s. a bushel of 60 lbs.

The cattle are poor, half-starved little animals, fed on anything they can pick up in the bare fields, and on the cut stalks of the bajri, which is neatly chopped or cut, so that not a particle is wasted. Their dung is all made into sun-dried cakes for fuel, and this is the universal practice in all parts of India. The cattle are generally so poorly fed that the loss to the land by this practice is not so great as one is apt at first to imagine. On entering a village the first industry which strikes the eye is the preparation of this fuel, kneaded into cakes of a hand-breadth with broken straw, and plastered on the outer walls to be baked in the sun. Near the towns this forms an article of ready sale, and troops of women are met, with piled basketfuls on their heads, coming in from the country in the early morning to find a market for it.

The village itself is occupied by the landowners, the cultivators, and the labourers, and by the village bankers or traders, and a few artisans. The houses are, with one or two exceptions, all built of clay, most with a little courtyard of their own, and all occupied by separate families. They are placed on a slightly elevated site upon the accumulated ruins of older buildings. Entering the house of a comfortable ryot, I found the outer part inhabited by the elder of the family; next to him was a chamber in which the cattle are housed at night; beyond that a small open court, about twenty feet square, surrounded by little chambers. In the hot weather the bedsteads are kept in the open, and inside when cold. A man with his son, the son's wife, and three children live here. He is a cultivator with a farm of five acres, which he and his forefathers have possessed for five generations. The house is built of clay and thatched with reeds, as poor as possible, but quite clean. Their food is grain made into bread, with a little butter (ghi) to season it, one pound and a half of bread being the daily average for each person.

In another village of 350 cultivated acres there were fifty Zemindars, or landholders, in a population of 402.

For the cultivation of the land there were thirty ploughs and sixty bullocks. Part of the land bears two crops in the year, so that the 350 acres yield 470 acres of crop. The management of the irrigation water employs a good deal of labour. From the Government canals here the water costs 6s. an acre when drawn *ad libitum* without lift, and 4s. when it has to be lifted by the cultivator. It is generally used in excess, and injuriously to the crops, when supplied without lift, and, as it is thus used most wastefully, it has been suggested either that the rate without lift should be considerably raised, or that it should never be supplied except by lift. The saving of water in the last case might be found to be ample compensation for the extra labour imposed.

Mr. Buck, then the head of the Department of Agriculture and Trade in the North-West Provinces, now the head of the Government Department of Agriculture, had established an experimental farm here, where we saw trials of native and foreign ploughs, sugar-cane mills, water-lifts, fanners for cleaning corn, examples of deep and shallow ploughing, forage-plants under irrigation, varieties of fruit-trees for distribution, the application of manures—the advantage of which to the neighbourhood cannot be doubted. In a country like India, where the native landowners undertake no such experimental operations, the Government, which is the great landowner, is obliged to take the initiative. A most instructive example of the improvement which may be effected by the aid of manure is shown on a tract of waste land in the vicinity of Cawnpore, which, on Mr. Buck's suggestion, was levelled and trenched and covered thickly with city manure at the expense of the municipality, and now repays them by a rent of £5 an acre, yielding to its cultivators three crops in the year—Indian corn, potatoes, and tobacco. Sugar-cane is also grown to a small extent, to be used green, and brings £30 an acre and upwards. It grows thick on the ground, and ten to twelve feet high. The cane, when ready, is cut into little squares, and eats like a pleasant sweetmeat, for which there is a ready demand. In such a position, and on land so highly manured, the value of water is immensely greater than when applied to poor land, unmanured, and far from market. In the one case it would be cheap at £2 an acre, in the other dear at 5s., but the Government with little discrimination makes the same charge in both.

CHAPTER III.

THE NORTH-WEST PROVINCES.

On the 14th of November we left Cawnpore for Agra, travelling 150 miles up the plain, most of it less fertile than I had yet seen, and much of it damaged by the salt efflorescence. There are many poor villages in this quarter, and the famine had been sore in the land. The contrast exhibited by the present poverty and the past magnificence is more instructive than agreeable; for we spent part of the next day in Agra, which has eleven square miles within its walls, in admiration of the beautiful architecture of the Fort and the Taj. They are both the creation of the great Mohammedan family which conquered India more than 350 years ago, the wisest and the ablest of her rulers—Baber, Akbar, Shah Jehan, and Arungzebe, the Great Moghul emperors. The Fort, which was also the palace of Akbar, commands the river and city of 150,000 inhabitants, and incloses within its walls (which are seventy feet high) a great space, a mile and a half round, with very numerous buildings, both ancient and modern. Entering by the Delhi Gate, and passing up through splendid approaches, we come to the Public Audience Hall of Akbar, which is very grand. Seated above in an alcove, he looked down on the armed princes, officers, and retainers who came to pay their homage. Within are courts and courts, each more charming and beautiful than the last. The apartments of the wives are of white marble, the walls and ceilings exquisitely pencilled with inlaid precious stones, representing the shape and colour of flowers—the lovely overhanging windows and little open terraces overlooking the Jumna and the more distant Taj. The bath-rooms are beautiful—all of marble, the ceilings and walls sparkling with little mirrors let into the marble. The beauty and extent of this inlaying cannot be adequately described. The Hall of silent audience opens on a terrace where there is a black flat stone, which was the throne of the Great Moghul. Below it is the Jasmine Tower of the chief sultana, recently restored. Near this the famous gates of Somnauth, carried off from Ghiznee by Lord Ellenborough, are stowed, old and ugly, and believed to be counterfeit.

The gem of the Fort is the Moti Musjid, or Pearl Mosque, exquisite in purity of taste and beauty of design. There is no colour, no figure, no image—the command that no graven image shall be set up for worship being literally obeyed by the followers of Mahomet. No Christian church I have ever seen can compare in purity of design with this temple. It is all of white marble, from the pavement of the large court to the top of the three domes. The beauty of the slight pillars carrying the smaller domes is as wonderful as it is lovely. On the summit at a great height, exposed to the tempests which strike across the plains of India, these domes have stood for 230 years untouched by storm or time. No lightning conductors are here to preserve them from the bolt which might in a moment sweep them away, and they now look as white, clear cut, and fresh as if they had just emerged from the hand of the builder. The mosque occupies a length of 124 ft. by 56 ft., the front court being about 100 ft. more from mosque to gateway. It is on the crown of the fortification, and was built by Shah Jehan, son of Akbar, in 1654.

We next drove down the river to the Taj, the tomb of the favourite queen of Shah Jehan. It is probably the most magnificent tomb in the world. We enter a gateway and drive some distance between long rows of low, Moorish, arched buildings to the grand gateway with a row of little domes on the top, which of itself would have been a monument of great magnificence. It only serves to usher you into a straight marble pathway through an exquisite garden terminated by the Taj, whose pure white marble dome, with its ivorylike tracery, is seen rising far above the verdure of the trees which line the approach to it. On leaving the path you rise by a marble stair and arrive on a marble platform, on which the whole magnificent structure appears to rest. Entering the building, you come to a circular marble screen, with exquisite tracery and inlaid flowers in variously coloured precious stones, inside of which are two marble sarcophagi, beneath which, in the vault below, the emperor and his wife are buried. That of the fair Moomtaz is distinguished by the words, in Arabic, "The name of the lady buried here is Moomtaz Mahal." Nothing more. You descend into a vault below, where similar sarcophagi are repeated, and in these the remains are inclosed. The whole building has been cleaned, and the minarets regilt. The feeling it inspires of beauty and majesty far exceeds that of the white marble cathedral of Milan; it is at once more simple and its form and tracery more elegant. It is said to have cost three millions.

One cannot help feeling that a race of kings like Akbar and Shah Jehan, who could illustrate their reign by such wonderful monuments, ought to have known how to rule this vast empire with advantage to its people. These buildings are the representatives of their civilisation and taste, and must have been the outcome of a feeling of security and peace. Long years must have been spent in their completion. What has become of the culture which is here displayed? We leave the Taj and drive back to the city, passing a few villages of agriculturists, lodged in their mean mud huts. How did these great men deal with their people? Akbar is said to have left a code of rules for managing the land and dealing with the cultivators which was clear and just. He and all his race have disappeared. Let us hope that the works of our modern civilisation, roads, railways, telegraphs, irrigation-canals, and navigable waterways, with security of person and property, will gradually enable the people to rise into a more prosperous condition, and be hereafter a better monument than they have yet proved of the beneficence of our rule.

In the afternoon, on our way to a famine-stricken village, we passed the tomb of Akbar at Secundra, about five miles north of Agra. In the grand gateway here, 570 wretched prisoners, whom the over-full gaol could not contain, were lodged, and were being taken out in batches for exercise. A more miserable procession it has never been my lot to witness—some, manacled on both ankles, carrying their chain; some with a manacle on one; all half-starved and very poor. Alas for us, that such should be the unhappy state of any fellow-subject! Some were seated in rows, and as the "sahibs" passed, at a signal from the keeper, gave a clap with their hands and a very hollow, cheerless cheer. The gaols at present are overflowing with prisoners for thefts, in consequence of the famine and high price of food. The tomb itself is much plainer than the Taj, and is chiefly built of red sandstone.

On reaching the village where we had arranged a meeting, the people came out to see us and to lay their tales of misery before us. Their crops had failed, and they had no credit, and the native bankers no money to lend. The death-rate had increased tenfold, and more were expected to die. The land was a rather light sandy loam, for which the occupiers paid 6s. an acre, one half to the Goverment, the other to the Zemindar—a not excessive rate if the fall of rain, or the supply of water, were sufficient. It had failed them last year, and twelve families had deserted their land and had not returned.

The growing crops had little promise, the cotton not 30 lbs. an acre. And so silent are these people in their distress that the settlement officer, who had been two months encamped on the land, had not observed any particular poverty, nor had become aware either that the people were in a state of famine, or dying of it. And to my astonishment the Government representatives here learnt all this for the first time, as the result of our visit.

At another place I visited the courts of law. In one the assistant magistrate was dispensing justice. Twelve persons had been tied up in a row the day before, and whipped with thirty stripes for theft. The magistrate said to me, with some satisfaction, that he had at last got a policeman who could break the skin at the third stroke! This, I am glad to say, is the only instance I met with in India of such a feeling. Whilst I was in court a man was being tried for attempting suicide by jumping into a well. For this he got a month's imprisonment. Suicide is very common. Another magistrate lately had a case of a man who walked into the Ganges and lay down to drown himself, but was pulled out. On being asked why he did this, he said he could get neither work nor food, and he thought his position not likely to be worse in any other condition after death. Upon being asked to promise not to repeat the attempt if let off, he said he would try for three or four days to obtain work, but if he failed he should have no other alternative. He got twelve months to compose his mind.

Under the present system in this part of India a re-settlement, or new tenancy, takes place every thirty years. The last change of this kind in the North-West

Provinces occupied several years, and cost two millions sterling. On being concluded the experience of the officers was dissipated by being turned into other duties not requiring this special knowledge. If re-settlement is to be continued it would be better to take it up, in a thirtieth part every year, by a special body of men who would become experts. And the increase of revenue would then be regular and annual, instead of by a huge jump at the end of the thirty years.

The prison at Agra, under the very intelligent management of Dr. Tyler, contained 2,375 prisoners, whose average weight when admitted compares unfavourably with that of 1875, there being a loss of 6½ lbs. per man, which he attributes to the recent great scarcity of food. There are very few female prisoners, and their comparative paucity in India is remarkable. The average prison population in Bombay is one to 1,815 of the general population, but that of the female prisoners is only one to 23,500 of the proportion of female population. This may be safely taken as an illustration of the proportion of female crime throughout India, and seems to indicate both the state of subjection of women, and the absence among them of crimes of violence in a country where intoxicating drink is rarely taken. The order and cleanliness in this prison, and in others which I visited in India, are most creditable to the management. Carpet-weaving seems to be readily acquired, and the prisoners generally are kept usefully busy. This prison is managed under Dr. Tyler by a sergeant-major of the artillery, who drills the most deserving prisoners as a night watch. Solitary confinement does not seem to be reckoned severe by the Indian people, who are quite content to be left quiet so long as they are regularly fed.

We returned next day from driving twenty-two miles into the country to see the general cultivation and state of the people, and rested for the night at Futtapur Sekri, a city of the great Akbar. It was built 300 years ago, and deserted in the next century on account of its unhealthiness It is walled, stands on a ridge of rocks, and is now occupied by a country population of 6,000. The palace is in good preservation; the buildings of red freestone beautifully carved.

As we entered a village early next morning the women were all going to the well to draw water for their daily use. The well is situated under the umbrageous shade of a stately pepul-tree. A raised platform, some six feet higher than the ground, circular, and ten or twelve feet in diameter, was the place from which the buckets were let down, and evidently the gathering-place for the morning gossip. Some were young and rather pretty, some middle-aged, all with silver anklets and bracelets, and ear and nose rings. Each had a large earthen jar and a smaller one, and a brass vessel. They let down the large earthen jar into the water, and filled from it the other, two, then refilled it, and placing the three on the edge of the platform descended the steps to the ground. In doing so they necessarily turned towards us. Each placed the large jar on her head, then with both hands lifted the brass vessel on the top of that, then took the small earthen jar in the left hand, and, so laden, stepped with stately mien on their homeward way. Like the servant of Abraham, I was tempted to offer my aid in drawing the water or lifting the jars, but not knowing the language, did not venture to do so. But the whole primitive story was recalled, and the people in these villages, and in their daily avocations, are but little changed from the time of the Patriarchs.

The tahsildar is the head native officer of the tahsil, which may include 100 villages and 80,000 to 100,000 people. He is the native assistant of the collector, and a magistrate. The desire now is to introduce natives of good birth to such offices; and the tahsildar's assistant who accompanied us is a man of twenty-five, dark, and not very smart-looking, but a lineal descendant of the great Akbar, and of the royal family of Delhi.

We examined a village eighteen miles from Agra, in extent 500 acres, of which 350 are cultivated. Population, 253. The lombardar, or headman, of the village has been sold up by a native banker, who eight years ago began to give him advances, and gradually, by increase of interest, having obtained a judgment for the debt, bought up his property—about the half of the village. We had the man before us, a member of the same family as the Ranee of Oudipore, of the oldest and highest rank in India. He is now a beggar, dependent on his neighbours for bread, without a particle of clothing beyond his loin cloth, and so poor and thin that he was pitiable to behold. As the other half of the village is pretty free from debt, there has probably been less thrift and industry in this family than the rest. But none of the people of the village looked prosperous.

On the following day we visited an indigo planter near Gazhibad, twenty miles from Delhi. This gentleman was an engineer engaged in the construction of the railway, and, when the Mutiny broke out, rendered valuable aid to Government by keeping the line open. When all was over he was rewarded by some of the forfeited land of the rebels being sold to him on favourable terms. He has 12,000 acres, but keeps in his own occupation only 100 acres. The remainder he lets to yearly tenants on condition that they pay him an adequate rent, and grow such crops as he prescribes. The crops were heavy, and the village people looked more cheerful than most I have yet seen. This landowner is now the only Zemindar or landlord on the 12,000 acres he bought. He lets his land on a written lease from year to year, reserving from his tenants all legal "rights of occupancy." His people pay much higher rents than the old rates, and are themselves more prosperous. The leading condition of his bargain is that he is to have a right to control the cropping. Every third year the tenants are to grow indigo where the soil is suitable, the crop of which he buys from them at a paying price. They grow also sugar-cane, and winter crops of wheat or barley. They have a full supply of irrigation-water from the Ganges canal, which is here a fast-flowing river, larger than the Thames above tide. They pay from 14s. to 18s. an acre for the land and water. He has tried English ploughs, but the people prefer their own, with which they plough the land repeatedly and make an excellent seed-bed. The indigo crop grown every third year runs its tap-root deep into the subjacent soil, and thus acts better than trench-ploughing. The indigo straw from the vats, when rotted into pulp, is laid on the land in large quantity, but, notwithstanding this addition to the ordinary resources of the soil, he believes the produce (under the exhausting influence of canal irrigation, which stimulates for a time but without enriching the soil) has sunk ten per cent. in twenty years. The deposit at the bottom of the canal is cleared out once a year. I saw it, and it seemed pure sand, and thus brings no reviving help like the mud of the Nile.

It seems incredible that, for twenty years after the Ganges canal was made, the natural drainage continued in most cases to be blocked by the canal embankment, which had been carried across the natural outfalls of the country, with no provision of siphons or outlets. The consequence was an accession of fever and the spread of rhé, both attributed to the canal irrigation, when in truth they were the natural consequence of water-logging the soil by blocking up its outlet. Meerut, it is said, was so desolated by fever, from this cause, that it had to be partially given up as a military station till this want of outlet was discovered. If it had not been for some independent planters, who were not afraid to speak out, the cultivators would have continued to suffer, seeing desolation, but accepting it as the destiny of fate through the ignorance of the Government. But where were the collectors and their deputies and assistants, whose duties lay specially amongst the cultivators? The amount of judicial work now cast upon them compels them to neglect the interests of the ryots and cultivators, and has indeed been one cause of that growth of litigation which now taxes the energies of so many various courts. If you ask the European officers the condition of the people in any village or district, they can seldom tell without making a special inquiry. The minor judicial work can be, and is, done by native officers, probably better than by English, because of their familiar knowledge of the language, habits and traditions, and general motives of their own people, and at one-fourth of the cost. If the whole detail of minor judicial work were left to them, with the adequate European courts of appeal now provided, and if the attention of the European officers were more confined to the condition of the cultivators and people, they would be in a position to prevent such oversights, and to keep in check the rapacity of native bankers, and to foresee coming scarcity in time to warn the Government to provide against it.

We have been riding about the country here on elephants in the hot sun. It is not a pleasant mode of progression, but the docility of the great animal is surprising.

Proceeding northwards through Meerut and Umballa, we pass large breadths of very fine sugar-cane under canal irrigation, the country clothed with fine trees and presenting general signs of prosperity. The Government assessment here is 5s. to 6s. an acre, with 10s. added for water-rate to the sugar-cane, which can well bear the charge. The Ganges and Jumna canals, valuable though they assuredly are, do not protect more than one-sixteenth of the area of the Doab, that being the proportion in which the canal water reaches the cultivated area. Outside of this, wherever there is a water-bearing stratum from which water-can be drawn at thirty to forty feet, there can be no safer investment for the capital of the cultivator, or the Government, than the construction of permanent wells, at a cost of £10 or £15, and capable of serving six acres, which on a system of three-course crops would admit of one-third of a holding of twenty acres being brought under irrigation every year. It is the opinion of many persons of skill that the water from such wells, notwithstanding the cost of working them, would yield quite as great a profit to the cultivator as that from the canals. Whatever may be the cause, men of experience here see little improvement in the condition of the cultivators. The great expenditure in railways and canals has left them much as it found them. The towns are improving, sanitary arrangements having rendered them more healthy, but this is entirely the work of the English. There would seem to be no public advantage in pressing great Government works, which are not required for public purposes, too much in advance of the wants or capabilities of this people.

CHAPTER IV.

THE PUNJAB.

We now enter the Punjab, the latest great territorial acquisition of the British Government in India, the school in which some of the chief of her more recent statesmen and warriors were trained, and notably the two Lawrences, Sir Robert Montgomery, Sir Donald M'Leod, Nicholson, and Edwards. The cultivated area of this province is twenty million acres, and the land revenue about an equal number of rupees, so that each acre on an average pays to the Government something less than 2s. But, in addition to the cultivated land, there is an equal quantity of culturable but uncultivated land, which bears part of this charge, so that if we place this at 6d. an acre the cultivated land will cost not quite 1s. 6d. There is, further, an area of twenty million acres of unculturable waste, which, so far as it bears any assessment, will still more reduce the charge on the cultivated land. Six per cent. of the cultivated land is irrigated by canals, besides that which is served by wells. The Punjab alone, with a population of 17,600,000, has an area in corn half as large again as that of the United Kingdom.

The general system of land-tenure in this province is that of village holdings, the headmen collecting the Government assessment, and paying it in one sum to the native collector. Each man has his specific land, recorded in the books of the village accountant, but the people are represented through their headman in their business with the Government. The machinery by which the Government acts may be shortly described. The native officer in immediate contact with the people is the village accountant, one in each large village or for several small ones. Twice in the year he takes an account of the crop in each field, and the changes, if any, of ownership and occupancy. He measures the ground at resettlement, subject to the revision of the European officer. There are fifty or sixty of these accountants in each tahsil or subdivision of a district, and they are the men in Upper India on whom Government rely for all information connected with the land. Their salaries are about £12 a year. Next over the accountant is a native superintendent, who supervises the work of the accountants for the whole tahsil, with a deputy to assist him. These are respectively paid £30 and £18 a year. Over them is the tahsildar, or native collector, to whom the revenue is paid by each village. Besides revenue duties he has also magisterial duties, and to the cultivators he is the tangible representative of the Government. His annual salary is from £200 to £300. The European collector, with his European assistants, controls the whole district, which includes eight, ten, or fifteen parts, or tahsils, yielding a revenue of from £50,000 to £120,000, and embracing a population of from 500,000 to 1,000,000. Within this district the collector is the supreme authority. He and his deputies and assistants are paid at a rate nearly tenfold that of the native officials.

The city of Lahore, the former capital of the Sikh rule, rises from the river Ravi, slightly above the general level of the plain, and is compact and more substantial than most Indian towns. It is surrounded by a wall, with the fort at one corner, and has a population of 90,000. The environs of the city, which were a waste when we took possession of it, have been turned into public gardens, very nicely kept, and with excellent roads for a mile or two in every direction. The country within some considerable range on each side of the river is richly wooded, and, looking down upon it from the fort, appears a really fine, rich country, well clothed with handsome timber, well cultivated, and capable of maintaining a prosperous people.

Market-garden farms begin outside the city walls, and are skilfully managed. I examined one, four acres in extent, served by a well twenty-two feet deep, which supplies water to every crop. The cultivators sow at the same time crops which mature respectively in three, five, and eight months, the shorter-lived crops coming to maturity before the longer ones have reached the size at which they would interfere with the others. They manure heavily with town manure, and have large returns, chiefly from vegetables and green fodder, sold in the city by the greengrocers. The Government revenue and cesses are about 20s. an acre. In a circle beyond this, several miles from the city, the farms are larger, a well having sometimes from ten to twenty acres attached to it. Such lands pay to the Government in revenue and cesses about 8s. an acre. The land is placed under irrigation in succession—about four acres each year, which is fairly manured, and, besides yielding a lucrative crop, leaves the land in a favourable state for dry crops till its turn for irrigation and manure comes round again. The unirrigated land pays 3s. an acre. Where the well is sufficient for the irrigation of most of the land held by the cultivator, the course he adopts on a ten-acre farm is to have two acres immediately round the well cultivated with tobacco and vegetables, and heavily manured. These are the crops that take most water and pay best for manure. Four acres outside these get less water and less manure, and yield two crops in the year—wheat followed by maize. The remaining four acres get whatever water and manure can be spared, and yield steadily an annual crop of wheat. The fields subject to the last two courses are put into each in turn. When such lands are underlet by the Government tenant, the rent paid to him for the irrigated land is one-third (the cost of cultivation being greater), and for the unirrigated one-half of the produce.

Out in the country, forty miles from Lahore, we walked through the land of a village of 450 acres, of which nearly the half was capable of irrigation by wells. Each well has two or three acres of high cultivation close to it, which usually begins with sugar-cane, for which the land is well prepared and manured. The rest of the irrigated land and the unirrigated is cultivated in the common course of Northern India—wheat followed by millets, and then ten months' fallow and ploughing, thus yielding only two crops in two years. The Government revenue and cesses on this land are about 2s. an acre. One particular holding of forty-two acres of irrigated land which we examined is held jointly by four brothers. They cultivate this themselves with the aid of six farm servants and their own sons, dividing the produce of each harvest in four equal shares. For this the Government assessment and local cesses amount to 3s. an acre. The farm servants are paid thus: they get two good meals a day; a coarse clothing, and 2s. a month in cash. The labourers' diet consists of unleavened cakes of whatever corn is in season, a little boiled peas and greens, with buttermilk, and sometimes a little butter cooked with the greens. The morning meal, between eight and nine, is usually of corn cakes with a pot of buttermilk, and the evening meal of the same kind of cakes, hot, with boiled pulse or greens. They eat on an average 2lbs. of flour and 4oz. of pulse per day. A ploughman, working hard on his own land from morning to night, will eat 3lbs. of flour. The cakes are usually of wheat and barley mixed, or maize or millet. The grain is ground by the women of the house in hand-mills of stone, of which we saw several in the house. The farm cattle were five pairs of bullocks for working the wells and ploughing, and six cows for milk. There were good supplies of grain and cotton, stored in earthen bins. The elder man owed his banker £20 at 18 per cent., for land bought a year ago. He expects soon to clear this off with the present high prices, and is, on the whole, a fair example of a Punjab agriculturist, a little better off than the average.

The Government assessment is fixed for terms which in some cases run for twenty, some for thirty years, the shorter terms being used on the lands most likely to be affected by the opening of markets consequent on railway extension. The Sikhs are a superior race, intelligent and outspoken. It seemed to me that they would readily follow a good example if some energetic European agriculturists were planted among them, farming this fine soil simply for profit, and using the means that capital and wider knowledge could command. But the low wages, and great number of people seeking land, would probably lead to a more profitable mode of investment. It is so easy to acquire the zemindar's right of property for a few years' purchase of the Government assessment, and the land can then be so readily sublet at a profit, that there is no advantage to be gained by entering into speculative farming. An Englishman embarking his capital in the purchase of land as a zemindar, and letting it on the native plan of a share of the produce, which he would then have an interest in bringing up to the highest point by liberal outlay as a landlord, might thus get a good return for his money, whilst largely benefiting the people. He could impose terms in order to prevent too great sub-division and its consequent certain poverty, and could betake himself to the hills in the hot weather. There is no reason why these fertile plains, under such management, should not display the same smiling picture of comfort and well-directed industry which gladdens the eye of the traveller through the plain of Lombardy, where the owner and the cultivator participate in the cost of improvement, and together share in the produce.

From Lahore we went towards Peshawur as far as Gujranwala to see the country, still the same great plain which for more than 1,400 miles stretches from Peshawur to the sea at Calcutta. In a village we met a zemindar who had fought against us at Sobraon thirty years ago, and is now a contented subject. He took us into his village and into the houses of his people. Their houses are very small. They use neither chairs nor tables, so that they require but little space, and in warm weather they sleep outside in their enclosed yard. Every one seems to have a store of grain. A small hand-mill is used by the women to grind their daily food, and thus the flour is always fresh, and ground with the bran in it. They knead it with their hands into a flat circular cake. This is laid on a pan and baked on the fire. This was a Sikh village, and though the people here, as farther south, are all very lightly clad, these seemed more cheerful and happy.

In walking through the fields where wheat-sowing was going on, the ground having been previously watered from a well, our party alarmed the two pairs of oxen which were drawing the two little ploughs, and they broke away in terror of the pale faces of the "sahibs." They were soon caught and brought back, and the master and his men with smiling good-nature asked us politely to be good enough to stand back, as they could not otherwise go on with their work. In another field where wheat-sowing was proceeding I was struck with the ingenuity of the sower. He performed the whole operation himself. He guided his bullocks and the plough, and into a short bamboo, which was fixed to the handle of the plough and passed down to the ground behind its sole, he trickled the seed from his left hand. It fell very regularly into the opening made by the plough, and was at once covered by the earth crumbling in over it as the plough passed on. The most perfect English drill could have done the work no better. He was an intelligent man, for when, forgetting that my language was not his, I asked him to show me the quality of the seed, he, understanding the action, at once placed a handful of it in mine.

There are three modes of irrigation in the Punjab—that of wells, already described, canal irrigation, and inundation irrigation. About one-fifth of the land through which the canals pass is supplied with water. The people may alter this fifth from year to year, so as in five years to bring the whole of their land under irrigation in turn; for the Government intention is that, to the extent of one-fifth, each holder shall be protected from drought, and this protection is being gradually extended over the country as funds will admit, but limited, of course, to the area over which a flow of canal water can be commanded. The inundation irrigation does not extend beyond the river basin. It makes the summer crop safe in most years, and, if the full river continues late, helps also the winter crop.

There are vast untouched tracts of jungle in this presidency capable of supporting any probable increase of population for many generations. These are great plains of alluvial land, in some parts of which there are remains of villages long since deserted, most likely from changes in the course of rivers having left the people without water. They are traversed by the five great rivers which unite with the Indus below Mooltan, and are capable of being reclaimed and rendered habitable by canal irrigation supplied from these rivers. The area so available may be counted by millions of acres, and it may soon become a question of policy whether the transplanting of the people to this, and other regions, from the too densely crowded countries farther south, may not be one effectual means of averting future famine.

The relations of the bunyia, or money-lender, with the cultivator, a question of the gravest character in India, have here been the subject of careful investigation. Some of the legal authorities, in order to limit his power, advised that land should not be transferable for debt, that a mortgage upon it should not outlast the life of the mortgagee without official sanction, and that so much of the annual produce of the land as represents the cost of cultivation should be exempt from attachment. It was found, however, on careful inquiry in this province, that the actual transfers had not been in excess of a natural and healthy process, and that the total number of suits for debt against the agricultural class was one in 125 annually, which is below the average of England. By a return for 1874–5, carefully collated by the Financial Commissioner, Mr. Egerton, now Sir Robert Egerton, lately the able Governor of the Punjab, it appears that only one landowner out of 540 had parted with his land, that the proportion sold for debt was less than two acres per square mile of the cultivated area, most of which was bought by agriculturists, not professional money-lenders. The average price was twenty-seven years' purchase of the Government assessment, and the greatest number of sales took place in the most prosperous districts. Only one acre in fifty was found to be mortgaged, and five-sixths of the land so mortgaged remained in possession of the borrower. Acting on these facts, a public meeting representing the landowners and their creditors, and the public generally, recommended that no further restraint should be placed on sale or transfer of land than would prevent fraud or undue advantage, and that any legal prohibition against usurious rates of interest would affect both borrower and lender injuriously, and diminish the market value of land; the fear being that the measures contemplated would tend to keep land in the hands of a succession of paupers.

In the museum at Lahore may be seen specimens of all the products of the province. Gold is found in small quantities in the sands of the Indus. Lead and iron exist, but no coal, only lignite. For clothing, cotton and silk are produced, and for food every variety of corn. Oil, sugar, and tobacco, are also largely cultivated. Where the land is unmanured the weight of corn produced per acre is about the same as that of unmanured land in England.

On Sunday I attended church in a tomb, said to be that of a favourite dancing girl of a former sovereign. This was then the only Protestant church in Lahore. The Governor's residence is a mosque of earlier times, very solid, with handsome square rooms, one of which is now a grand dining room, opening from a suit of drawing-rooms.

Umritsur, with its golden temple and fine country, was our first halt on leaving Lahore. Here again were complaints of the waterlogging of the land, consequent on the embankments from the Baree Doab Canal. A case was mentioned to me where a cultivator came to the Commissioner with a chafing-dish, filled with fire, on his head, to demand justice for injury to his land done by the Sircar. After much time was lost the matter had been inquired into, and the damage done to these poor people by having their drainage blocked by the canal embankments is now being rectified. But the appointment by routine of a weak, or indolent, or incapable man at the head of a district, is quickly followed by laxity on the part of his under native officers. And the evil this may cause to a population of several millions is frightful. Great indeed is the responsibility of the men who make such appointments.

The Rev. Mr. Clark, who has been a missionary in the Punjab since 1851, called on me here, and gave me very interesting information on missionary enterprise in this part of India. A high-class Christian school has been established for native converts who are being prepared to become missionaries among their own people, the management having been undertaken by young Englishmen of fortune who are devoting themselves to this work, Mr. Baring at Batala, Mr. Bateman, and Mr. Gordon taking the lead. The Zenana Mission is considered as likely to prove the most successful branch of the Christian Mission, the converted native women having great influence with their own people.

The European officers have much influence, and would gladly use it in protecting the people, but they are too generally moved about so much from one station to another, or so closely confined to office work, that they have not time to become thoroughly acquainted with their stations. Their representatives, the tahsildars, or native collectors, if they cannot get the revenue otherwise, will in extreme cases sell up every head of stock and every bushel of corn, and even the very beams of the man's house, and put him into confinement for two or three days. Such powers, they say, are in many cases indispensable to obtain payment.

On the 25th of November we left Umritsur and proceeded to Kappurtulla, a native State in the hands of a little Rajah of six, who is under the superintendence of a British resident. The child Rajah lives in a house apart, going to his mother, the Ranee, every night. The resident lives at the Rajah's palace, a very handsome house, with busts in the hall of the Queen and Prince Consort, and Lord Canning, and pictures in the drawing-room of the Prince and Princess of Wales by Sant, and of Sir Robert Montgomery. A force of 500 infantry, with cavalry and artillery, was being sent by this State to Afghanistan, and we were invited to inspect them, a train of elephants with gilt howdahs, and cloths of scarlet and gold, being placed at our service. The Resident here, who has been a settlement officer and is familiar with our system, finds the rate of Government assessment on the land half as much again as in British territory, while sales of property under mortgage are very few. The Government keep the bunyias more in order than we do. The higher revenue officers, having smaller districts, know the headmen of all their villages better. It is only in this respect that the Resident would change anything in our management for theirs; but this better knowledge of the headmen, if possessed by our European officers, would give them a clearer insight into the actual condition of the people.

Crossing the plain some miles beyond the town, I found much of it rendered barren by the rhé, or salt efflorescence, generally ascribed to canal irrigation; but, as there are no canals in this State, it cannot arise from that cause here. The mud houses in the first village we came to had been to a large extent melted by the late heavy floods of this season, many inches of rain having fallen in twenty-four hours. The people were busy rebuilding their dwellings, which are neither better nor worse than those in British territory. The people looked exactly the same—their average holdings, six to seven acres. The only crop which received no injury from the flood was the sugar-cane, which, so long as it can keep its head above water, remains uninjured by it. Near the city the land is richly cultivated, and lets as high as £4 an acre for garden-ground. The principal minister, a native, who accompanied us in our ride, was minutely acquainted with the condition of the people and their modes of cultivation.

In the evening we left for British territory at Jallundar, and thence proceeded to Roorkee, where we were very kindly received by Major Brandreth, who is in charge of the college for engineers here, which, with the Government workshops, we visited in the afternoon. I here got my first view of the Himalayas, with a grand snow-clad peak, 22,000 feet high, topping the rest of the vast wall that shuts in the great Indian plain. There is between us and the high range a lower range of hills, but they scarcely seem to intercept the view of the mighty ridge beyond. The great plain seems a dead level, shut in by the mountains, from which it has in long course of ages gradually crumbled down. As the sun set the nearer hills had a rosy hue, and the distant snowy mountain-peaks shone out sharp against the sky.

We had a most interesting trip to Hurdwar, which is the first point where the Ganges leaves the hills and enters the plain. The river is here embanked along its various streams and all collected to one point, where, according to its fulness, the necessary volume is passed into the canal, and the rest is left to run onwards in its natural course. At this time (November), and for the next five dry months, nine-tenths of its waters are taken into the canal. When the rains set in, and the snow begins to melt on the high mountains, one-tenth will be sufficient. The canal is a stupendous work, worthy of a great nation desiring to protect its passive subjects from famine. The principle upon which it is constructed is to lift part of the water of the Ganges from its natural bed, and run it by an artificial channel along the watershed of the country, whence it can be allowed to flow through the adjacent country by irrigation channels, to secure the crops from drought. The canal is a great deep river, flowing at the rate of one to two miles an hour, and in the course of its first twenty miles from Hurdwar it is passed *below* two wide beds of torrents, *through* one, and *over* a fourth, all with extraordinary engineering skill. It was designed by Sir Proby Cautley, an artillery officer with a great genius for engineering, and is a monument of his talent. It carries the water for 260 miles through the rich Doab, or flat country between the Ganges and Jumna. The snow-melted water is at a temperature of 60° in summer when the air and the surface of the ground are 110°, and this coldness of the water is at that season sometimes injurious to the crops. A great canal, such as this, carried along the watershed of a country, must, by percolation, raise the water stratum over all the land commanded by it, and thus greatly increase the irrigation-power of wells.

Near Hurdwar, which is the holy place to which all Hindus endeavour to make a pilgrimage at least once in a lifetime by themselves or their representatives, we met many of them returning, carrying away a bottle of the water of the holy river. We rode on elephants through the town. When we reached the top of the high, broad flight of stone steps, down which the pilgrims go to bathe, the huge animals stood still for a little, while we looked down upon the scene. To my astonishment they then in single file slowly descended the steps, and walked into the river among the bathers, and the sacred fish which swim in swarms at this point. No one seemed surprised. We crossed a little arm of the stream, and ascended some steep and broken ground, which the sagacious creatures managed without difficulty. As we looked down from the height to which we had then reached, a dead man was seen floating past on the broad stream. About a mile farther up we left the elephants and returned by boat, and were rowed swiftly down the river, passing the temples on the river-front, from which they looked much finer than from the road behind them. But the reality is not to be compared with the pictures of these buildings; for really these temples are mean-looking and all out of repair. The grandeur is in the great river and the gap in the mountains through which it passes out, and in looking towards the profound distance, towards the great Himalayan chain whence it comes.

The engineering college at Roorkee has three classes —the first for the higher branch of engineering, the second for secondary work, and the third for mechanical operations. The numbers now admitted are restricted, as there is not employment for the young men who could be turned out both here and at the Engineering College at Cooper's Hill. The workshops, under Mr. Campbell, turn out all kinds of articles for Government use—military and engineering tools, agricultural implements, hand-pumps, sugar-mills, machinery of various kinds. He finds native labour, at any work except farm-work, as dear as European. The people have no liking for piece-work, at which they might earn higher pay. They say that hard work makes them ill; and what advantage is it to earn more than suffices for the day? When they quarrel, which they often do, they don't fight, but they damage each other's work and make charges against each other, the truth being difficult to elicit. I was informed by the magistrate of the cantonment, a military officer who has been many years in the country, that nine-tenths of the cases are mere squabbles that might be much better settled at home than by dragging people for miles, and detaining them for days at a court of justice. The people are like children, constantly squabbling, and they go to law, get up false evidence, and do all sorts of tricks for mutual annoyance, which the existence of our courts facilitate and the pleaders encourage. A punchayet, or native court, he thinks, composed of a headman from each adjoining five villages, meeting once a week at each village in succession, could settle all petty cases and put a stop to the chief part of the present litigation.

At Delhi we were the guests of the Commissioner, who lives in a handsome house outside the walls, called Ludlow Castle. In the grounds of this house was planted, at the Mutiny in 1857, one of the batteries that crumbled the walls near the Cashmere Gate; and behind it is the ridge on which lay the small English force—at its greatest 7,000 men—which, during the terrific heat from June till September, had to take a walled city held by 60,000 rebel native soldiers. We passed in through the Cashmere Gate, which, with the broken wall, is left as the siege left it, and saw the spot where the brave young engineer officers, Home and Salkeld, fastened the powder bags to the gates and applied the fire, when one was killed and the other fell mortally wounded into the ditch. Nobly seconded by their sergeants, two of whom were killed, the gate was blown in, and the assaulting column rushed up under General Nicholson and captured that position. We followed the gallant Nicholson's course along the wall inside to the spot where he fell mortally wounded, General Pelham Burn being beside him at the time. We went through the fort, the palace, and the city, and finally to the tomb of Humayoon, five miles out, where the King of Delhi took refuge, and whence he and his sons were dragged out from the midst of thousands of their followers by the brave Hodgson and his men.

Then we drove seven miles farther to the Kootub—the highest tower in the world, built 600 years ago, of red freestone, and in the most perfect preservation, and wonderfully symmetrical and beautiful. We went up to the gallery on the first storey, and got a splendid view of the country, which, all the distance from Delhi—eleven miles—is a succession of ruined cities, palaces, and tombs. It must at one time have been in a far more flourishing condition than at present, and doubtless this splendid, elegant, and massive tower will see many generations yet—some, let us hope, recalling the grandeur of its earlier time. There is an archway close to the tower, said to be the most beautiful in India, of red sandstone, beautifully hewn and carved, inlaid with marble, with four arches and a splendid dome.

On the 1st of December I rose early and walked out with Colonel Davis to the "Ridge," a long space of elevated, rocky, broken ground, behind which, in 1857, our troops lay whilst waiting for reinforcements. It was here in a night attack that Colonel Robert Yule was killed. His is among the names inscribed on a tablet in the memorial tower, erected here in memory of the brave men who fell in the siege.

The weather was beautiful, like a lovely summer morning at home. The country all round is covered with park-like trees, and has a rich and luxuriant appearance. The Indian cork-tree is in flower, with delicate pendent petals and pretty white flowers. There is also the acacia, with its yellow flower and sweet perfume. From this point we drove through the centre of the city into the Queen's Park, which is very pretty, extensive, and well shaded, with open ground for cricket. The military band plays once a week, and the native public resort to it in great numbers. The park is open to all, and is entered from the principal business street, just as you might go out of the Strand. At one end of the park is a museum, with specimens of produce, and natural history, and antiquities, and with a large library. There is also a chamber for the municipality of the city, whose representatives, under the presidency of the Deputy Commissioner, transact the public business. The population of Delhi is 160,000.

In the evening I walked over the land of one of the cultivators, who was busy in his market-garden in the environs of the city. The ground had been waste, covered with large stones. The municipality set to work and had the stones taken out, and the ground trenched and well filled with street sweepings and manure. It is now let at 40s. an acre. The tenant readily answered every question. He has a well sixty feet deep, from which he waters his land. It is worked by four oxen, which do the other work of the farm besides. The ground grows all sorts of vegetables and flowers for sale in the city—two crops in the year, corn and vegetables in succession. The effect of the manure is expected to last for ten years. This man cultivates fourteen acres. He employs five men, who are paid 10s. each a month, with vegetables besides. They work all days of the week, except one holiday every new moon. He has a fine crop of cauliflowers now on the ground, which he sells at 2d. a head. His well supplies water for twelve acres, some of the crops getting eight waterings. The man was very intelligent, and appeared an industrious, careful fellow—a Rajpoot—but bare-legged and bare-footed, like others. No Englishman or Scotchman of the same rank could be more clear and business-like in his explanation.

It is the opinion of the Commissioner that a better division of labour might be made between the British and native officials. The native judges are quite capable of transacting the most of the legal business of the country, subject to the appeal courts, and to such aid as the British officers could give, in the cold weather, and also in the hot weather, when it is not possible to work out of doors. The European officers would then have time to become really acquainted with the people in their villages and farms, the district officers being the ever-present representatives of a careful, paternal Government. The people, as a rule, live so close upon the edge of want that constant watchfulness is necessary. If the collector of a district had, with the consent of the Commissioner of the division, power to suspend to some extent the Government demand in bad years, making up for it in good seasons, the poor cultivator would be rescued in large measure from his dependence on the money-lender, and tided over to the next crop. For it is rare that both crops of the same year are lost by drought. When the monsoon rains fail in summer there is generally a good winter crop.

The dried cow-dung brought into Delhi, and sold for fuel, fetches, for a buffalo-load of 4 cwt., 2s., equal to 10s. a ton.

CHAPTER V.

NATIVE STATES.

FROM Delhi we proceeded to Ulwar, a native State, with a population of 780,000, where a young man of twenty rules under the guidance of an English political agent. We saw his Highness's palace, his stud of 300 horses, comprising Arab blood of pure strain, and his elephants and camels, and finally his wild beasts—all very princely. The country is no longer the great plain of India. The capital is 1,000 feet above the sea, and the fort which defends the city is behind, and 1,000 feet above it. The position is very picturesque. The city is walled, and full of active, busy people, more so than in British India generally, and with more sign of life—having the advantage of a reigning prince resident, who spends his income at home. Behind the palace is a spacious public park, and, beyond that, the fine temples and tomb of a former Maharajah.

There are three classes of people in this State, as distinguished by their food, in the proportion of four, sixteen, and eighty per 100. The first consume, without stint, milk porridge, ghi, sugar, and good flour.

The second have buttermilk porridge, a little ghi, no sugar, and only coarse grain. The third have only water porridge and coarse grain. About one-half of the whole area is under cultivation, and nearly one-half of that is irrigated. Coolies earn 3d. a day, carpenters 6d., and masons 7½d.

The villages and farming are inferior to those in our territory, though the rate of Government assessment is higher; and the country being of a sandy nature, the drought has told with terrible severity, many villages having lost half their people, and working cattle, from famine. A certain amount of help was given to the famishing, but not with the same feeling of responsibility or to the same generous extent as in our possessions. Twenty per cent. of the whole population have died or emigrated, and fever is very general and fatal, owing to the bodily weakness consequent on scarcity. The money-lenders have ceased making advances to the cultivator, the security being gone for a time.

Next day we reached the native State and city of Jeypore, the country still flat, but with picturesque hills dotted over its surface. We drove through the public gardens, which are very handsome, and then through the city, which is surrounded by a strong wall. The city is laid out in parallel lines, two great streets, each two miles long, perfectly level and straight, being crossed at right angles by narrow streets. The population of the city is 170,000, that of the State two millions. The great streets are very wide, with fine pavements at each side for foot-passengers. The houses are built with some degree of regular irregularity, all of pinkish colour, with every variety of elevation, and the prettiest little balconied windows dotted along their fronts.

One block of the city, being one-eighth of its extent, is occupied by the palace of the Maharajah—a vast structure or series of courts and buildings, the innermost of all being the residence of the prince and his family—a fairly large one, seeing that, besides nine wives and their attendants, he had two thousand women in his establishment. We first ascended by a long rising pathway, winding up till we reached the roof, where there is a little marble canopy and pillars, under which there is shelter from the sun, and whence you command a panorama of the whole scene. It was like a scene in a play, or from the "Arabian Nights." Gardens stretched away, filled with servitors of the palace—men and women, walking about among beds of flowers and grass—fountains playing, and at some distance a fine pond; beyond it a larger one like a lake, on which a small pleasure steamer is kept; beyond that woods and palm trees, and a water palace some two miles out, with a still larger lake stretching to the ridge of precipitous hills, 1,000 feet high, that shut in all approach on that side of the city, except at one point, where a huge gateway closes or opens the only pass. Turning round, the eye follows this line which shuts out the outer world, and shelters inside of it gardens and houses, and at the opposite end is guarded by forts on conical hills that meet the ridge behind the city. On the top of it is the fort of Jeypore, 2,000 feet above the sea, 800 feet above the city. The sun was making the finest effect of light and shade on the purple-coloured hills, refreshed by the sparkling verdure of the trees on the plain.

And what is to be said of the absolute ruler here, with power of life and death over all his subjects? We were met at the door of the Reception Hall by a little man in spectacles, with a large diamond in his hair on the top of his head, and a pretty posy of flowers in his side hair, to whom we were presented. After shaking hands he led us in, seating himself on a sofa with myself and the other gentlemen seated right and left of him, and a large number of his court standing round. I complimented him on the beauty of his palace and city, and the grand elements he had contributed for the health and comfort of his people, in air, light, and water, by the wide streets, the gas lamps, and the water supply. To this he replied by a polite bow. We then rose, he again leading us to the door, and courteously taking leave. He seemed sad and depressed, and has since died.

Before breakfast we drove eight miles out to examine the country and the public works of the State, which are under the management of Captain Jacob, who has been eleven years here, and has constructed all the roads and irrigation works made during that time. He lays a report and estimate before the Maharajah, who, upon approval, places the amount at his disposal, so that no after interruption in the execution of the work occurs. The complaint in our territory is that works are begun, then delayed for want of funds, and when completed are proportionately costly. The plans and superintendence here cost 6½ per cent. on the expenditure; in India, I was told, the cost greatly exceeds that amount. The cultivated land is a light sandy loam, into which any rain that falls sinks, and does not run off. The rent paid to

Government for such of it as is capable of irrigation by wells is 12s. an acre, and 6s. more for water when supplied from irrigating channels. Sometimes the Government rent is paid in kind—a proportion of the produce. We met a row of some eighty bullocks carrying the Government rent of a village, in bags of corn over their backs, into Jeypore. Though the assessment is much higher than in British India for similar land, the people seem in no worse condition. They are never allowed to be sold up by the bunyia, neither their land nor working cattle. Within a few miles of Jeypore the land becomes very sandy, and a large tract of this is kept in a wild state for hunting antelopes and pigs, where sometimes a tiger also is found.

Next morning we passed through an encampment of natives, and were forcibly reminded of the Scripture, "two women grinding at the mill." There they were sitting on each side of the circular stone, and with great quickness grinding the flour for the day's repast.

We were on our way to Ambair, the ancient but now deserted capital of Jeypore, and seven miles distant from it. After leaving the plain we mounted elephants, which took us over the Pass and down into the gorge where the old city stands. The people have abandoned it, and it is rapidly going to ruin. There is a lake at the bottom of the gorge, with an island and gardens upon it. Two alligators were sunning themselves on a bank, one within stone-shot, which darted swiftly into the water on being soundly bumped on the tail by a stone. The city is surrounded by walls, and the great palace is still habitable, and stands above the lake on the lower ridge of hills, behind which on a higher point is a very extensive fort which commands the city and all its approaches. The elephants took us up the steep stone ascent, and into the main gate and court of the palace, where we alighted and spent an hour in traversing its storey upon storey of apartments. Our kind host, Col. Benyon, had provided a luncheon basket, which was opened under a fine canopy of Jade-like marble pillars. Thence we passed into a series of beautiful apartments, decorated in the purest taste, the walls grey in colour, with an intermixture of what shone like mother-of-pearl, and with little mirrors inserted regularly throughout. The cornices and ceilings were quite exquisite. The rooms were perfect in shape and proportion, 30 feet by 17, with little outer chambers on the external walls, whence, through beautiful marble trellice-work, you look down from the great height on the lake and gardens, and the surrounding hills. From the roof itself, which is of easy access, there is a still more extensive view. The zenana, now empty, is divided into cells, in which no life could appear to be more solitary or uninteresting. From these we descended to a temple, where still, every day, a goat is sacrificed to appease the Divine wrath; and on certain great occasions, when the Maharajah is himself present, seven buffaloes are beheaded with the same object—"Not without blood." After leaving the temple we remounted our elephants, recrossed the Pass, and returned home in the moonlight.

We now took rail for Ajmere—ninety miles—which we reached in seven hours. This is one of the State lines, made by the Government on a cheaper scale than the great guaranteed lines—about £6,000 a mile, narrow gauge, and very comfortable; everything finished in the best style, with good stations. At Ajmere, which is the central station, great engineering shops are being constructed for the repairs, with a little railway town springing up around it. When the line is completed to Ahmedabad, there will be a direct run from Delhi to Bombay, shortening the present journey by nearly 400 miles. But between Ahmedabad and Delhi there is a break of gauge, which must greatly impede the heavy through goods traffic, and is a most erroneous economy on a great through line.

At Ajmere we were hospitably received by the commissioner, who lives in a pretty house placed on the edge of an extensive lake, bounded on the opposite side by high and rugged hills. Ajmere itself is 1,800 feet above the sea-level, and these hills 800 more; so that we are on the backbone of Central India, the water now flowing west. This place is quite lovely. Above the city is a still higher hill, rising 1,200 feet. It is like the better class of Indian cities, and possesses a very sacred Hindu temple, at the door of which we were met by all the principal priests, and each presented with wreaths of flowers. Behind this temple is a deep abyss with a spring of water at the bottom, whence the people draw their supplies. A little on one side are the ruins of what is said to have been the finest Hindu temple in India, covered in front by a façade of Moslem architecture of wonderful majesty. A Mahometan conqueror ordered the Hindu temple to be thus converted to the true faith, and took this means of doing it. Both are now only splendid ruins.

In our drive we passed the Mayo College—a new building, erected by the Rajpootana chiefs for the education of their youths of princely birth—at present under the management of Captain Loch, on the principle of an English public school. Each chief has built a residence, or "house," for his party, and, as they are all different, and all near the main school, there is much variety and beauty in the whole. I saw the boys out playing lawn tennis. They play cricket also, and are thus being brought up with manly English habits, though not to despise their own people, but if possible to carry to their homes a portion of that English love of truth and fair play which may serve them as chiefs hereafter. The drive all the way was on excellent roads, lined with fine trees, with plenty of shade. In the evening there was a party at the Commissioner's house, where, among others, I met Mr. Brandeis, the Inspector of Forests, and Mr. Halsey, the Salt Commissioner, from both of whom I derived much valuable information. On returning to my room the moon was shining on the rippling waters of the lake which my windows overlooked, and I recalled to memory the story of the Veiled Lady of Ajmere, which I had read in an annual forty years ago.

Next morning I saw Mr. Grey, the missionary here of the United Presbyterian Church of Scotland. The missionaries of this Church, like the American missions, associate with them a medical missionary. By their schools, more than by preaching, they find influence among the people, who are kind and patient. During the late famine the mission rendered active help by giving employment and wages in making wells, and thus employing the famishing people profitably without breaking up their homes in relief camps.

The Sambre Salt Lake in this neighbourhood is the source of salt for Northern and Central India. The quantity to be had here and in the river Loony is unlimited. This river falls into the Gulf of Cutch, and for many miles near its outlet the salt is very pure and fine. Millions of tons of it are yearly washed away by the sea in the Run of Cutch. Mr. Halsey has lately visited this almost unknown country, where he found an isolated but strong race of people inhabiting a fine stretch of land, cut off by sandy deserts from the rest of mankind. By recent fiscal changes, and arrangements with native independent chiefs, the monstrous hedge, or Customs line, has been abolished, and by approved appliances the cost of getting the salt has been largely reduced. This saving will be an important service to the State if it enables the tax to be reduced, and adds another million to the revenue without imposing any additional charge on the consumer.

Leaving Ajmere at night, we returned through Jeypore to Bhurtpore, which is a tract of light, sandy country, and a salt-producing State. Thence to Jhodpore, with a population of two millions, and a revenue of one million sterling. If British India were capable of being managed at the same rate, she would have a revenue of upwards of a hundred millions sterling. The hills soon disappeared, and we again enter the great plain of the Ganges. The most obvious feature of difference in the appearance between the native States and British territory is the greater prevalence of trees in the latter. Mr. Brandeis, the Inspector-General of

Forests, tells me that his department is preserving existing forests and preventing their waste, but they have found it too expensive to replant the ground. Nor is it necessary, for Nature, if she is left to herself, soon covers the ground with new trees in those forest tracts where they had been wasted. With this object these are enclosed, in stony ground among the hills by stone dykes exactly like ours at home, and, in places where there is not this resource, by the prickly thorn—Euphorbia—which quickly springs up and makes an impenetrable hedge. A most singular provision of nature seems thus to exist for the preservation of trees, and thereby securing moisture and shade. This prickly thorn spreads rapidly over all uncultivated ground, and the birds flying about drop seeds of trees among its branches. Some of these reach the ground, and, in the rains, take root, and out of the midst of those wide-spreading prickly thorns, which no animal can penetrate, springs a young and lusty tree, which has thus been guarded from all danger in its early period of growth.

The poverty of the cultivator makes him very dependent on the native money-lender. The first pressure that drives him to seek this aid is the prompt payment demanded of the Government assessment. It is fixed for a term of years, and must be paid whether the season is good or bad. If the season is bad, and the crop partially fails, he has no help but in the money-lender, the bunyia. Many devices have been thought of to relieve him, one of which seems to have much to recommend it. Let the Government assessment be so much money in the aggregate for ten years, with a power in the hand of the collector to suspend collection in bad seasons and double it in good. The present assessment may be very low, but in a bad year when there is no surplus, a man with no capital has nothing with which to pay it. When a productive year comes, the assessment is so moderate that the surplus will readily answer the double demand, and the poor cultivator will then be able to meet his engagements to the Government without having incurred the ruinous rates of interest which would have otherwise been charged by the money-lender. This would in reality be a modified plan of Government banking, but applicable only to the payment of the rent or Government assessment, and involving no further risk or detail of management on the part of the Government.

The system of Government advances called Tuccavi, for the purpose of enabling the landholder to make wells or other permanent improvements, is so overloaded by precautions in the shape of forms and stamps, and application to the courts, and the employment of paid agents, and delays, all which cost the borrower a very large proportion of the whole advance, that comparatively little use is made of it.

The collection of the revenue itself is becoming more difficult from the constant growth of judicial work. The Tahsildars, or native collectors, who are also magistrates, find the judicial work more dignified and attractive, and a shorter road to promotion. They now move about their circles with less frequency, and are becoming less acquainted with the character and condition of the people. And the same is the case with the English officers who supervise them, but who, from the great increase of appeals, are detained in their courts, and are obliged to subordinate the far more important duty of acquiring a personal knowledge of the people themselves, to this discharge of judicial functions. This has become aggravated by the elaborate procedure introduced in recent years, by which cases which might have been disposed of satisfactorily to both parties in two or three hours, now occupy more than an equal number of days. Thus the business of Government is becoming enormously hampered and increased by the introduction of legal principles and practice suited to entirely different circumstances.

In the native States I have observed little difference in the condition of the people as compared with those under our own rule. On the whole they seem to have more solid and permanently constructed villages. But in both there is the appearance of a uniformity of poverty. But we must not judge this people as we should do at home. They have few wants, a few shillings will clothe them, and a penny halfpenny a day, with ordinary prices, will feed them. Their only ambition is to dower their daughters handsomely according to their station, and with this object, and in entertainments at the wedding, they generally spend four or five years' income. This they borrow from the village banker, to whom, as a rule, they are all in subjection. Their industry at seed time and harvest is untiring. But when they have done their best then, and in watering the growing crop, they are content to be quiet, and will sit perfectly happy, doing nothing, all the rest of the time. The Hindu religion is a belief in a great and dreaded unknown Power, whose wrath they desire to appease. Power of any kind they seem to deify, and, if the British had accepted their worship, it would have been readily given to an authority they feel, but do not comprehend. In approaching you they clasp their hands together, and with humility advance as if in worship. They are naturally a quiet, docile, simple people, who have never for long ages known anything but bondage, and they look upon us as conquerors who desire to be just, but don't know how to do them justice.

CHAPTER VI.

NORTH-WEST PROVINCES AND OUDH.

WE now re-enter the North-West Provinces and Oudh, which contain a population larger than that of France. Compared with the cultivated area, this province is the most populous in India, 420 to the square mile. To maintain such a population, with no other important industry but the cultivation of the land, is of itself a proof that the soil must be fertile.

Before leaving Lucknow to examine the country, I traversed the city, and the scenes of British valour which have given it an imperishable name. The Residency so long defended against the rebels, the room in which Sir Henry Lawrence received his death-wound, Dr. Fayrer's house in which the hero died, the Baillie guard so nobly held by a small body of faithful Sepoys, are all now kept neat and trim as a garden, though the ruins still show the mark of the shot and shell unsparingly rained upon them. I saw also the house where Havelock died, and his tomb at the Alumbagh, and the enclosure within which a large body of the rebel soldiers took shelter, whence none escaped alive. Now all is peaceful. There are great open spaces where houses have been demolished, to leave free range for guns. But there seems danger near this large and unquiet population in having no fortress in which to make a stand against sudden attack. The roads and gardens and public parks surrounding the city are most extensive and beautiful, but the 400,000 inhabitants care little to participate in their enjoyment.

The Talookdars of Oudh were originally either hereditary landowners or the King's collectors, and each of them had many villages under his charge. When we annexed the country, the Government dealt directly with the cultivators through the head men of the villages. This aroused the vigorous animosity of the Talookdars, and at the mutiny many of them joined, probably encouraged, the outbreak. The heads of the villages or petty zemindars, whom we had intended to secure by our policy, left us at once and joined their former chiefs. When the mutiny was quelled, the ancient system was reverted to, the Talookdars were replaced over their villages, and the small zemindars were reduced to the position of under-proprietors. There are thus three stages of tenure: the Government, as superior; the Talookdars, as equal sharers with the Government in the land revenue; and the under-proprietor. The Talookdars receive a thirty years' settlement (by which the Government assessment is fixed for that period) on the principle of one-half the surplus rent being paid by them to the Government. The other half they share equally with the under-proprietors. It is held by the courts that, under the grant made after the mutiny, the claim, termed an "occupancy right," to hold the land after undisturbed possession for twelve years, cannot now be forced upon the Talookdars. The cultivators are thus either "under-proprietors" or tenants at will.

The Talookdars, whose position for political reasons it has been thought necessary to sustain, had many of them since the mutiny, through extravagance and mismanagement, fallen into such pecuniary straits, that an Encumbered Estates Act was passed for their relief. But they were not treated like our Irish or Highland proprietors, whose estates where sold away from them, and the price divided among their creditors. The Government took these gentlemen under its charge, advanced large sums of money to compound with their creditors for cash, undertook the management of their property, giving them a moderate income to live upon, until by careful nursing the estates should be cleared of debt and restored to them free. Any success that has attended this is to be attributed to the extremely favourable terms on which these lands are held from the State, coupled with the substitution of honest and strict management in the place of native extravagance. This aristocracy has not as yet altogether answered its purpose of standing between the Government and the cultivators, and capable of helping their people in times of drought and famine. Many of them, notwithstanding the great advantages granted to them, have been obliged to come to the Government to save themselves from ruin. To this there are exceptions, and one of the most notable is the Maharajah of Balrampur.

His estate comprises 2,500 villages, for which he pays the Government a fixed annual rental of £80,000, for a term of thirty years, when the rent will be subject to revision. He has the sole control of his tenants, who are all tenants at will, but are never displaced if they fulfil the written conditions under which they hold. The collection of the rent is let to farmers, in lots of about five villages to each. They cannot displace any tenant, nor change the customary rents. These are taken in kind, one half of the produce, and as cash is not required, the cultivator has no occasion to borrow from the bunyia. The Maharajah employs fifteen Tahsildars, or agents, who manage the several districts, and who, being magistrates, dispose of all disputes, so that there is no other litigation among the people, and no appeal to other courts of law. He has early notices of approaching drought or scarcity from his officers, who are constantly among and are acquainted with the people; and either retains grain in his stores, or if that is not likely to suffice, buys at once as much as he deems necessary, and keeps it ready for distribution. To the cultivators he advances what they want, to be repaid when they can afford it; and to the others what they need, getting some useful work in return. He has a form of agreement with his tenants, of which he gave me a copy. It is clear and precise in its clauses, and provides reasonable compensation in case, for any reason, the tenancy is brought to a close.

The Provincial Governors complain of the deadening influence caused by the interference of the Governor-General's Council, each member of which has a special duty confided to him, and thinks it necessary to question all suggestions from the subordinate Governments. In Lord Dalhousie's time business was much better accomplished when details were left to their superior local knowledge and experience. The Civil Code, too, has introduced pleaders in the small-debt courts, who harry the poor. The bulk of all litigation could be disposed of by native judges, and, if the European officers had time to know the people better in their villages, much of it would never arise. In regard to famine relief work, the opinion of men of much experience here was that such works could only be profitable when carried out by the strong and able-bodied; and all others should be succoured at their homes.

On the 11th of December I joined the Commissioner's camp under the trees near a small town, in the country of the Talookdars of Oudh, having left Lucknow in the early morning, and after a drive of some miles, and a subsequent walk through the country, arrived here at eleven o'clock for breakfast. After passing through the rich land which surrounds the city, and which resembles a finely-wooded English park, we come to an open flat country, with no trees, which is covered with water in the rains, but is now carrying the spring crop. Passing this, we find again the usual cultivation. For the first six miles we met troops of people bearing their burdens to market, most of the men with bundles slung over their shoulders on their long heavy bamboo staves; the women and boys carrying on their heads baskets loaded with dried cakes of cowdung, which they sell in the city for fuel; some with vegetable or dairy produce. All are very lightly clad, but earnest in the work they have in hand. Many heavily laden two-ox carts press on towards the same market. At the eighth mile we are met by a carriage accompanied by horsemen. This is the Talookdar of the district, who alights, and we alight to meet him. He presents a gold mohur, which is touched, and we shake hands. This is an acknowledgment of his being subject to the Queen-Empress; and he considers it his duty to render her officers aid whilst in his country. We part with him on leaving the road, and, walking through the fields, we come to a dry gheel, covered with short creeping grass, and find several women busy "grass-cutting." They have a short sharp knife in their hand which they sweep in front of them, half cutting and half scraping the short grass clean off the surface. The roots are left undisturbed, and soon grow again if there is dew or moisture. There is heavy dew on the grass as we walk through it. A woman or lad can soon make up a bundle of this grass weighing about forty pounds. Thirty pounds is the daily allowance for one horse, with eight pounds of small beans or other corn. The forenoon's work yields about threepence. The owner of the grass gets nothing, and it is the custom that any one may go grass-cutting wherever he sees a suitable locality.

Walking on through the fields we come to a well which the cultivator is working with two bullocks, and the aid of two nice-looking young men, his cousins. He is troubled when addressed by strangers, but soon takes courage from the kindly tone of Major Erskine, and tells us his story. He has twenty-five acres of his own, as an under-proprietor of the Talookdar, and holds five acres besides as a yearly tenant. He pays the Talookdar five shillings an acre for the former (of which the Talookdar pays half to Government), and twenty shillings an acre for the latter. The land is all of the same quality, and the difference of cost marks the relative rate of holding as an under-proprietor, and holding as a yearly tenant. His crops are good and well-cultivated. With "well irrigation" he gets 1,800 lbs. of corn to an acre in good seasons. The well is a small one, with no permanent brick lining. While we look on, the edge upon which the water-skin is emptied has softened, and suddenly shows signs of giving way. The wood framing is quickly removed, and the ground slips into the well, but not much of it. The three men are handy, and quickly replace the broken face by planking, and again rig up the well with its lift, and start the bullocks and recommence the work of irrigation. The whole is done in a sensible, business-like way. The men are hereditary proprietors.

In the afternoon we walked through many farms in the neighbourhood, and I was glad to find such excellent crops of all kinds, and generally so rich a country. The small farmers seem very industrious, and the land is well managed. In feeding their bullocks and cows they show great good sense. We found each man preparing the evening meal for his stock, on their return from the scanty pastures. They draw the green mustard plant from among the growing wheat, chop it up and mix it with chopped haulm of the bajri or coarse corn, and so make a palatable and cheap provender. The cow manure is here, as everywhere, dried into cakes for fuel. When asked why they did not reserve it for the land, they answered, "What would you? We cook our food with it, we warm our bodies with it, and then we use the ashes for manure." They are very quick; a Brahmin boy of fourteen followed us about—he pointed to a fox stealing away among the corn. "Why don't you run after it?" "I could not catch it." "Why not?" "Because it has four legs and I only two," smilingly said the boy.

On these fine rich lands the growing crops were all good. Sunnai, hemp, eight feet high, is grown for its fibre, chiefly for the manufacture of ropes, and for seed. It yields about 1,000 lbs. of dry fibre to the acre. The jowar and castor-oil plant were so tall and strong that I could not touch the top of either with my whip from horseback. I measured an average stalk of jowar, which was fourteen feet high, and all cuts into good fodder. Potatoes are largely grown, and are a fine crop. The rent of this land paid to his landlord by the cultivator, if a tenant at will, runs from 20s. to 30s. an acre.

Here I must record an incident which is characteristic of the people. In walking through the fields I observed that we were constantly followed, at some distance, by a suspicious-looking native. It seemed impossible to shake him off. As the groups from each village left us when we quitted their bounds, this man perseveringly followed. I asked an explanation. He was a man against whom the Commissioner had decided a civil suit some weeks before. It was a decree on a bond which took away his land. He was dissatisfied, and adopted a practice which it seems is not uncommon. He had followed the magistrate some forty miles, sits all day near his tent, follows him wherever he goes, says nothing, but hopes by this means to procure some change of judgment. This seemed to me intolerable, and I requested a gentleman of the party, who combined muscular strength and firmness with an admirable gentleness of demeanour to the natives, to intimate to the man that force would be used if he did not at once retire. He accepted the hint, and for the time disappeared.

We shifted camp next morning, and rode on some fourteen miles further to breakfast, spending the time in examination of crops. The neighbouring Rajah, after presenting himself, asked us to pay him a return visit at his Castle. So at four o'clock in the afternoon our party mounted two elephants, and rode through the town to his abode. It is finely situated on a high bank—a large, straggling, pretentious house, with a mixture of tawdry finery and unfinished rooms, which is the common characteristic of a wealthy native's dwelling. After going through some ceremony here, we walked on to his balcony, and saw a splendid piece of farming stretched out on the plain below. On returning home we passed through this, and found it chiefly tobacco of most luxuriant growth, poppy for opium newly sown, sugar-cane, jowar, and other crops. These grow on a large flat of fine alluvial land of several hundred acres, which in July and August is flooded by the river Goomtee, the rich deposits of which leave an annual increase of vigour. No farming could be finer, or more free from weeds. It was quite garden culture. Five wells, the water pumped up by oxen, were pouring their refreshing streams, carefully directed, among the crops.

In the evening, about ten, my secretary* and I

* Now Colonel E. Pemberton Leach, V.C., R.E., to whose knowledge of the language and people, and his tact in eliciting information, I was much indebted.

started in "Palki Dawk," which means that each was carried in a long coffin-like carriage, at full length, as in a bed, wrapped in our great-coats, for a five hours' journey to the nearest railway station. We had forty men, including a mounted sowar or swordsman as guard. Four men at each palki took turn and turn about in carrying us at a trot, and a torchbearer ran alongside each carriage. We crossed a ferry on the river, and were laid down about half-way till some dispute among the men was arranged. About half-past three A.M. we reached the railway, by which we proceeded to Fyzabad.

The country towards Fyzabad varies from poor to good. The poor is in waste grass, useful for stock, and the good is land watered from wells, and showing every prospect of good spring crops. The sugar-cane is very good. In some places four or five men are doing the work of the oxen in drawing water from the wells, and, wherever there is a hollow in which water stands, it is being carefully lifted and distributed over the crops. The herds are few, many cattle having died during the late scarcity, and both men and women are therefore working the wells. This part of Oudh is not richer than the average of the great Indian plain. Groves of mangoes are frequent. The young trees are planted about twenty feet apart in squares, and are carefully protected by strong grass tied round them. The remarkably luxuriant crops of jowar and dhall are attributed to the land having had rest for a year, the previous crop having entirely failed from drought. In the near neighbourhood of Fyzabad the land is very highly cultivated, and yields, in some cases, £7 an acre of rent, under potatoes, for sale to the Europeans, and from tobacco, or opium. There has never been potato disease, and the crop is very profitable. An old and experienced Rajah told me that the land, except where manured, was losing its productive qualities by constant cropping, as the luxuriance resulting from a year's rest in fallow clearly showed; and that this was the general opinion of the cultivators, though the deterioration was so slow and gradual as not to be easily perceived. The people are improving in their circumstances, the railway having opened up new markets. Six years ago the Deputy Commissioner had occasion to make special inquiry into the economical position of the cultivators, and there was not one that was not in debt to the Bunyia. This year, on repeating the same inquiry, he found not more than fifty-three per cent. in debt. There is a prevailing opinion here that there is a great future in the land, that the revenue must increase at each new settlement, and that time and good management will bring all successfully round.

Much complaint is made of the needless labour thrown upon district officers by the secretaries of the General Government, in requiring minute explanations of matters which have already been examined and disposed of by the more competent judges on the spot, the superior officers in each Presidency, whose decisions are thus retried. This leads to an immense increase of desk work, and by so much interferes injudiciously with the local outdoor work, already heavily curtailed by increasing judicial labour. India seems to suffer much from the secretaries, men of ability and clever with the pen, some of whom, for these convenient qualities, rise to high positions without the opportunity of gaining experience out of doors, or any accurate knowledge of the people. As there is neither parliament nor public opinion in India to criticise or control them, and as their influence in questions of promotion is great, they possess a power not only quite beyond that of official persons in the same position at home, but greater than that of our parliamentary heads of departments. The interference which they thus exercise is very properly creating a strong desire for independence and separate self-government by each Presidency, and cannot be too soon placed under some effectual control.

The sub-Himalayan plain, the country lying all along and nearest to the mountain range, is underlaid by a water-bearing stratum, arising from the heavy rains in the mountains, which finds its outlet here along the whole length of the North-West Provinces and Oudh. The water is so near the surface that in average years even sugar-cane needs little irrigation. But in seasons of extreme drought famine has been occasioned, as no provision has been made for "well" irrigation. It has been proposed to carry the water of the rivers by canal along this district. But water being so near the surface it is believed that "well" irrigation might be made at less cost, and without the evils which often attend canal irrigation in this part of the country. It was the east section of this belt that suffered most in the famine of 1874, at Derbunga, and the west section in 1877.

There are special products other than those which directly feed the people, towards which the attention of Government has been engaged, with the view of developing industries suitable to the soil and climate, and which in their value, and cultivation, and manufacture, might create wealth, and give employment, beyond the common processes of agriculture. Of these, sugar, tobacco, and opium are as yet the most important, and indigo and jute, tea, coffee, and chinchona, are spreading in suitable localities; and silk has been successfully introduced in the valley of Dehra Doon, which is 2,000 feet above the plain. The silkworm is sent thence to the hills in the hot season, and brought down in March to hatch, when the mulberry leaf is ready.

Fyzabad is an ancient capital of Oudh. The most famous temple of the Hindus is at Adjudija, six miles out, on the banks of the Gogra. Here Rām, their great prophet, was born, and millions of Hindus every year make pilgrimage to the sacred birthplace. He dates 200 years before Christ. His birthplace was desecrated by Baber, the Mahometan conqueror, 300 years ago, who changed it into a Mahometan temple. In that state it still remains. But to prevent dispute the Commissioner built a wall to separate the birthplace from the temple of Mahomet, and so secured to each of the rival pietists their reasonable share of the sacred ground. There is nothing grand about the place except its position, and the reverence borne for it by its devotees. Monkeys in great numbers run along the walls and about the courts, and no one interferes with them. The country round is rich and beautifully wooded.

At ten p.m. we returned to our railway carriage, and lay down for a night's rest. In the middle of the night we were hooked to a passing train, and in the morning we were approaching Benares. This is one of the holy cities of India, with a population of 176,000, and is situated on the Ganges, after it has received the streams of the Jumna and other large rivers. In order to see it from the river we took boat, and were borne slowly along the front of the city, passing the numberless flights of stairs down which the people come to bathe in the sacred stream. There are temples, and princes' and great men's houses, along the bank, and the scene is highly picturesque. We saw several corpses brought down *into* the water, preparatory to being burnt, and one floating on the water. Leaving the barge, we then ascended by many steps to the streets of the city, which are narrow and rather unsavoury lanes, through which two can hardly walk abreast. The houses are high, the lower floor let in shops, and the upper storeys of the best inhabited by wealthy Hindus, who, after making wealth, come to die in the holy city.

A Rajah and native landowner here, who had had experience and rank in the Government service, was freely communicative of his views. English rule will, he says, commence its downfall when natives, either Hindu or Mahometan, are entrusted with leading positions. The natives, in his view, are centuries behind the English, and as the latter are constantly learning and advancing, it is vain for the natives to hope ever to equal them. What the people of India desire is not only the protection which our government gives, but the rest which they find under it. They are slow to learn, very conservative by religion and nature, and sadly put out by the constant legislative changes. If the English would only do nothing but govern, seeking no speedy changes, but being content to let civilisation gradually grow, they would be very popular. The wisest governor would be he who would rest, and let them rest. The most beneficial works ever done in India he considers to be the railway and telegraph, both of which are highly valued by the natives. They are very suspicious, and fear any novel proceedings of their foreign masters, whom they, therefore, try to propitiate, as they make offerings with the same object to their God. When an officer goes out to examine the country, they at once anticipate a new demand, and consider through what channel and to whom they can safely make a present to get an official friend on their side. Most native officers are believed to be approachable in this way, and each must get a share. Knowing this natural feeling of their countrymen, the native officials readily avail themselves of it by encouraging the idea that approaching enhancement of rent or other demands are at hand. In times of famine, and so long as it lasted, this gentleman would prohibit exports of corn of any kind from India. There is enough every year raised within it to feed its people; no import is required, and if export were forbidden the price would not, in his opinion, rise to an extravagant pitch within India itself. I visited a village belonging to this gentleman eight miles up the river, and saw many of his tenants. One of them is a thrifty, prosperous man, who, having saved money, is now lending it on the security of the land to his poorer and less industrious neighbours, and is rapidly buying up their rights. In due time he will become a comparatively large sub-owner, and they his tenants or labourers.

The Hindus, the Rajah informed me, have three castes: the Brahmins or priestly caste, the Shatrafs or soldier caste, and the Cultivators. To these a fourth is added, the Out caste, serfs or labourers. These are in the proportion, in each hundred, of ten of the first, ten of the second, thirty of the third, and fifty of the last. To the welfare of the first fifty the arrangements of Government are chiefly directed, and when their condition is prosperous, so, it is expected, will be that of the labouring class, who work for them, but have no land of their own. Water must not be touched in cooking by any but a Hindu, otherwise it is unclean, and a man would be turned out of his caste if he partook of it. Some men would die rather than do anything that would make them lose caste. It is this difficulty that prevents men of high caste from undertaking a long sea voyage, during which it would be impossible to prevent such contact as would injure caste. If a railway should ever be made to connect India with Europe, this difficulty would disappear, and many Indian gentlemen would then go to England.

We left Benares at 6.30 on the morning of the 15th December, and arrived at Ghazeepore, forty-six miles, at 10.15, doing the distance in the shortest time I have ever travelled by posting. Part of it we timed for four miles, at sixteen miles an hour. We changed horses five times, and were horsed through by the Maharajah of Benares, whose half-bred Arabs went most of the way at a hand gallop, a pair in each carriage. The coachman never left his box, but sat giving orders till the new horses were put on, and then quietly moved away, increasing his pace as we proceeded. He had excellent "hands," and drove with the greatest care compatible with such speed. The country for some miles was rich and luxuriant; the road as smooth as possible, hard in the centre, and not metalled on the sides, where the unshod bullocks with their heavy carts jog slowly along. From side to side it was over one hundred feet in width, shaded by splendid mango trees, which always yield shade, and, in time of fruit, most of their sustenance to the native travellers. In other places there were fine tamarind trees. The wide road, with its beautiful shade and luxuriant foliage, could not be matched in the richest parts of England. Cultivated fields, covered with growing crops, stretched away across the plain as far as the eye could see, interspersed with grand park-like trees in full foliage. The young wheat and barley, about a foot high, was being watered from the wells by the diligent agriculturists, and their docile little white bullocks. The green dhall, about six or seven feet high, and the solid fields of sugar-cane, eight or ten feet high, betokened a rich and generous soil, from much of which a previous "rain" crop of jowar, and grain, had already been reaped.

Village after village we flew through with John Gilpin speed, the two syces behind the carriage shouting out to the astonished inhabitants to stand clear. The elders bowed their heads in meek submission to this swift demonstration of visible power, the younger rushed to cover, the poultry escaped within an inch of their lives, and the lazy curs, suddenly aroused, had not time or spirit to give us even a parting growl. We come to an open country, with rice fields, and presently to ravines, which are always found near the great river banks. Our speed is diminished. We descend to the bed of the Goomtee, where we are followed by half a score of men from a hut on the road-side. This is near its junction with the Ganges. We cross the Goomtee on a bridge of boats, and on reaching the other shore, the men, at a signal from our active coachman, all join in a push up the steep bank, which we thus surmount without a pause. Taking a minute's breathing space for hurried instructions to our escort to return for the same help to the second carriage, our Jehu is off again along the level plain at a hand-gallop. I would back the Maharajah's coachman and cattle to go ten miles against the State Railway, at its usual pace, for any moderate amount.

We are now in a beautiful house, on the high bank of the Ganges, the hospitable residence of the opium agent, Mr. Rivett Carnac. This is the headquarters of one of the two great opium stations of India. It takes all that is grown in the North-West Provinces and Punjab, and part of Bengal. The growers have to obtain a licence from the agent to permit them to cultivate it. From the factory on the side of the Ganges it used to be shipped to Calcutta, but it is now sent by rail. The growers use their best land, obtain advances from Government, and must deliver all they grow at the Factory at a price fixed beforehand. That price gives them a larger return than anything else they grow except sugar, and yet it leaves a very large profit to Government. Each ball or "cake," as it is called (though when packed they look exactly like cannon balls), contains nearly four pounds of pure opium, closely packed in dried poppy leaves, and is worth about £3. Here they make a million such balls a year, from which the Government draws two millions sterling of profit.

These balls are put into chests, and sent to Calcutta, where they are sold by auction, and the purchasers, not the Government, ship them to China at their own risk. The opium grown in India is of finer quality than the Chinese, and so long as its quality maintains that pre-eminence, the Chinese demand will probably continue, and the revenue from this source, which is nearly one-eighth of the whole revenue of India, is not likely to be reduced. In its manufacture it gives employment to many thousands of well-paid natives, yields a handsome profit to the Indian farmer who grows it, and in its careful cultivation forms a good preparation for the following crops.

What had been the stud farm here has been converted into a tobacco farm, for which purpose it has been let to an English company. It is 800 acres in extent, good deep red land. A few villages in the Indian fashion have been run up to keep labourers on the ground, and each small holder is bound to put to the extent of one-fourth of his cultivation under tobacco. An American planter from Virginia is employed to superintend the manufacture of the tobacco when it comes into the factory. He says that the land here is much better than that of Virginia, and the crop, therefore, heavier. But here they must supply by irrigation the water which the climate gives there. It is got from tanks as long as they hold it, and by pumping from the Ganges when the tanks are dry. The greater dryness of the atmosphere may be a difficulty, but, from the experience he has had here, he believes that tobacco of as good quality may be produced as in Virginia. Labour here is less costly, six people being hired for the same cost as one, and they are quite as expert as the negroes. The tobacco can be grown and manufactured here at a total cost of not over sixpence a pound, and it sells at present for two shillings. The produce of an acre is 700 to 800 lbs., so that there is a good profit. It is being extensively and increasingly grown in other parts of India, and yields handsome returns for good management.

Before leaving the North-West Provinces, I must refer to the division of Jhansi, where there is great distress. This is due in part to inferiority of soil, though at an earlier period of its history it is said to have been a flourishing district. The cultivators are very poor, and it was thought that the want of capital, which is the common lot, might be made good by giving them the power to borrow on the security of the public land. A law was passed which conferred a continuing right of occupancy, with power to mortgage or sell. The poor people, who never had industry or thrift enough to save and value capital, thus found themselves suddenly in a position to command it, though at ruinous rates of interest, by offering this new security to the native bankers, into whose hands they speedily fell. The land is passing from them, it is becoming overrun by kans grass (a gigantic twitch) from their inability to cultivate it, and they have fallen into such a hopeless condition of indebtedness that special legislation to restore the former system is contemplated. And, as an immediate remedy, it has been suggested that a Government agent should be empowered to set aside the "remorseless action of the civil courts," and summarily to settle all accounts between the people and the bankers, the district having become disorganised.

A legal gentleman who called on me, a Pleader before the Courts at Lucknow and Calcutta, thinks that the higher education now being given to the people of lower caste will in fifty years make it impossible for us to hold the country.

CHAPTER VII.

BENGAL.

Crossing the Ganges, and travelling some forty miles further south-east, we reach Behea, having now entered the great province of Bengal. There are believed to be twelve million ryot holdings in this Province, one-half of which yield less than 10s. each of yearly rental to the proprietors. The latter pay to the Government, under permanent settlement, £3,600,000, and receive from their tenants £13,000,000, or nearly four times more than they pay. The difference, upwards of nine millions sterling a year, is not the whole cost to the Government of the permanent settlement, for thousands of acres of fertile land are left in jungle, in many parts of the Presidency, from the inertness of the descendants of the fortunate zemindars to whom the public property was made over, for a quit rent, about a century ago. The object of introducing a class of large proprietors was attained by elevating the revenue agents to that rank, but overlooking the interests of the ryots, who for the most part were the real landowners of the country, subject no doubt to the uncertain demands of the

Government. The cultivated area of Bengal is 54,600,000 acres, which (reckoning the double crop) is four times the extent of the corn and green crop land of the United Kingdom. Besides feeding a population double that of ours, there is an annual export of produce through it of the value of upwards of twenty millions sterling. The average price of cultivated land is from £2 to £6 per acre, according to situation and quality, subject to a Government land-tax of a penny up to eighteen-pence per acre. Field labourers' wages vary from twopence to sixpence a day, the latter rate being common in the villages of the Presidency division and in those of Dacca and Chittagong. When wages are paid in kind they are more uniform, being from four to six pounds of grain a day.

Near Behea we visited an estate of 20,000 acres, reclaimed twenty years ago from jungle, and now under fine crops. It is let on a beneficial lease for fifty years, by the Government, to Messrs. Burrows, Thompson, and Milne, who reclaimed the land, and have settled numerous small tenants upon it as cultivators on ten-year leases, with no "occupancy rights," and no power of mortgaging their land. The land is quite flat and well wooded, a fertile, easily-wrought, reddish loam, and watered by the Soane Canal. The people pay 8s. to 10s. an acre for the land, and 3s. for the canal water. They grow rice, sugar cane, opium, oil seeds, wheat, barley, and vegetables, all of the most luxuriant appearance. They manufacture the sugar themselves, by simply passing the cane through iron rollers, which squeeze out the juice, and this they boil in a flat pan, heated by the "trash," or haulm of the cane. The sugar crop yields a clear profit, after all costs paid, of £4 to £10 an acre. Mr. Milne, a Scotchman, who has been here twenty years, says that the small farmers, who live in mud huts built by themselves, are more comfortable and independent not only than our agricultural labourers, but than our small Highland cottier farmers. They are quite as intelligent in business as cultivators, for they do all the varied operations themselves. He finds them very fair in their dealings, and very tractable if they see they are fairly dealt by. There is still much good land farther south, suitable for English capitalists, equally capable of improvement, and with water advantages.

The climate is now sensibly warmer than it was in the Northern Provinces, and the palm-tree and rice cultivation begin to prevail. The plains covered with rice fields are at this season bare and bleak, and more treeless than other parts of the country. The land on the Soane is of a more sandy nature and reddish tint, and not so rich-looking as that of the Ganges plain. There are trees here, as in the North-West, called Mohawah, which yield a fruit that dries like a raisin, and then is converted into spirit. It also yields oil from the pulp, and the pulp itself may be likewise used for food.

After inspecting a manufactory of sugar-cane mills specially in use by the small farmers, we embarked on the Soane Canal in company with Colonel Haig, R.E., the Engineer-in-Chief for Bengal, and Mr. Levinge, the resident engineer of the works. We steamed some fifteen miles into the country, getting out at various places to see it. The canal itself is a splendid work, and in the engineer's opinion has made this part of Bengal quite safe from famine.

We found the rice crop being harvested. It was various in yield; some not over 400 lbs. an acre, some over 1,200 lbs. It is reaped with a sickle, the reapers sitting on their heels, and laying it down in sheaves, which later in the day are tied up and then placed in bundles of about twenty sheaves, tied neatly with a thin straw rope, and all carried home every evening on the heads of the reapers. Nothing is left loose in the field. We followed it to the threshing floor, and here seven oxen in a row, tied together, were walking over it round a fixed centre, and treading out the corn, the oxen "not muzzled." A little further was the heap, previously threshed, being winnowed by being skilfully held aloft and lightly shaken in the wind, while the chaff and dust were blown away. In the outhouse of the owner was a woman husking the rice, by standing on the end of a pole balanced so that the other end gently hammered the grain and separated it from the husk. In another outhouse was an ox grinding oil-seed for the supply of oil to the family; and still further, but out of doors, a small sugar mill pressing the sweet juice from the cane, which was then poured into the heated pan, and evaporated and boiled into sugar. All these various industries we saw going on amongst these intelligent villagers, all of whom seemed to have their own special work to do.

On my way home I called on Mr. Drummond, a brother of the late Mr. Peter Drummond, of Stirling, the famous tract distributor, and an old friend and constituent of mine when M.P. for Stirling. This gentleman has been fifty years in India, is seventy-eight, and has thus a right to speak with the weight of great experience. He had enjoyed good health, likes the country, had always been an up-countryman, and knew the feelings and habits of the people well. He gave me his opinion of the natives as skilful agriculturists, though poor, and a good quiet people, though with some not commendable qualities. They are quite ready to adopt new crops when proved to be remunerative, a remarkable instance of this being the rapid increase of the sugar crop, which has grown from a produce in this district of 28,000 to 280,000 maunds in three years. The great evil is the facility given to incur debt, and the difficulty is to find out a manner of utilising the indispensable Bunyia, without so much limiting his legal remedy as to create the need of more stringent terms on the borrower. Time, patience, and the higher prices of produce, will, he believes, ere long render the cultivator more independent. The intelligence is there ready to be utilised. Mr. Drummond, as the result of his long observation, has no belief in the theory of the exhaustion of the soil of the Great Indian Plain, which still, in a fine year with seasonable rains, and an occasional fallow, yields splendid crops of every kind. The old gentleman was much pleased to see me, and said he would let them know at home that he had had a call from "the Member."

The Soane Canal, when completed, will cost over three millions sterling, and will be capable of irrigating over one million acres. To pay 5 per cent. and working expenses, a charge per acre will be required of 5s. All the better class of land can afford this easily, but it may be found heavy on the poor land, and therefore a charge proportioned to the benefit derived will probably be adopted. The great zemindars under the Cornwallis settlement, who leave their rich jungle land in its natural state, pay nothing, as they refuse the water, though it would increase the value of the land tenfold if it was cleared and cultivated. Whatever may be said of the principle of that settlement, the inconsiderate haste with which it was carried out, and the want of regard for the rights of the cultivators, has in more than one shape entailed a heavy loss on India.

The collector and magistrate here has a district of 6,000 square miles and two millions of people under his charge. He has daily reports from his officers stating the fall of rain or otherwise, the appearance of the crops, and the state of crime. It is quite a small kingdom, over which he reigns supreme without a parliament, but responsible to his Commissioner and the Lieutenant-Governor. To this position, which for the due fulfilment of its various most important duties demands powers of no ordinary kind, the Civil Service claim right of seniority in appointment, a claim which, in the interests of the people, ought not to be listened to.

We left Arrah on the morning of the 18th of December, but not before paying a visit to the house, now historical, which was the scene of the famous siege during the mutiny in 1857. Mr. Boyle, an engineer, with prudent foresight, had stored it with provisions and ammunition on the first news of the outbreak. Three regiments of mutineers marched upon it on their way to the north, expecting it to fall an easy prey. All the English at the station took refuge in this house, Mr. Wade, a civilian, taking the command. They were six men in number, with twenty Sikh soldiers who stood by them. The English posted themselves on the principal floor, the Sikhs holding the floor below. Within a hundred yards stands a larger house, which was seized by the enemy, where they placed two guns, which fortunately burst soon after opening fire. For three days the besieged party held their ground, hoping every hour for relief. But water failed. Boyle set the Sikhs with their bayonets to dig a hole below the cellar, which fortunately yielded water! In the night they made a raid outside and captured some of the rebels' sheep. For ten days they held the place, killing many of the enemy without losing a man themselves, and were then relieved by a force under Sir Vincent Eyre. Six Englishmen and twenty Sikhs against 3,000 mutineers. Wade got for this splendid deed a C.S.I.! Boyle was more substantially rewarded. The house is a small two-story bungalow, the ground quite flat all round, and with many fine park-like trees. We were lodged within 150 yards of this house, with every door now open all night, as is the common practice in this country.

Soon after passing Beheah, we crossed the river Soane—on the longest stone bridge in India, I believe—at this dry season consisting of two small streams flowing on each side of its wide bed. We passed Dinapore, and Patna, where there is an immense granary, which was built many years ago as a safeguard against famine, but never used. The country is richly cultivated, with many temples and tombs among the gardens and potato fields. The land is beautifully managed, in fine fields of tobacco, linseed, and the small squares of poppy for opium. Palm trees are now seen overtopping every woodland, many single, some in avenues. Vast sweeps of verdure stretch away from the railway in the rice districts, gram and other late corn crops now in many places covering the ground from which the rice has been carried. The plantain, with its broad shining leaves, throws its cooling shade over the workers at the wells. Parrots and other birds of gay plumage perch on the telegraph wires. Verily it is a goodly country, from Mooltan to Calcutta a splendid plain of good land, for 1,600 miles.

At the next station we left the main line, and went a few miles down to the Ganges, where the agent for the railway had kindly provided a steam launch. The Ganges here is of great width, and much nearer the level of the land than I have yet seen it. When in flood it overflows much of the country. We steamed across and down the river for eight miles, passing about a score of alligators basking on the sand. Entering a train on the other side, in three hours we reached Derbunga, passing some very fine fields of tobacco on the way, much rice, and a fine crop of pulse everywhere. This was one of the worst affected districts during the famine of 1874. As a famine relief work the collector planted mango and other fruit trees along the sides of some hundred miles of the public roads, which, besides now affording welcome shade to the weary traveller, are capable of yielding food for six or eight weeks to tens of thousands of people, good and palatable when eked out with a little rice.

There are two lines of railway proposed for the north of this district, 114 miles altogether, which would pass through a populous country, tap Nepaul on its richest side, and have a large paying traffic. The country is level, no tunnels nor large bridges are required, and the land is cheap. In this locality the line could be constructed at £6,000 a mile, inclusive of plant. There is here, and in many other parts of India, an excellent opening for railway enterprise if conducted on principles of strict economy. Though the financial position of the Government prevented new works being then undertaken by them, the advantage they would reap directly, as the great landowners, in having access to markets opened up to their tenants, besides the greater safeguard against famines which railway access secures, might justify the risk of offering a partial guarantee upon well-selected lines. The State lines already made by Government are in fact as much guaranteed lines as those termed "guaranteed," for they are made with borrowed money for which the Government must pay interest. A better policy might be to induce capitalists to take this business into their own hands by offering a partial guarantee, on a specified expenditure, sufficient to give a basis of security, without lulling that activity and care which are necessary to the complete success of such an enterprise. Three per cent. consols are now almost at par, and while money is so cheap it seems not improbable that an offer of a three per cent. guarantee by Government would induce capitalists in this country to come forward, provided, under proper restrictions as to rates, the entire profit beyond the guarantee were left to them. Lines of railway made in this way through tracts of country as fertile as those to which, without any guarantee, British capital is sent in America, and with the great advantage over America of an abundant population fond of moving about, could hardly fail of success. The Government would be relieved of details for which it is not well adapted, while continuous work of construction would be secured, and men thoroughly trained in the business of transport and traffic management would be substituted for officers without such training.

In front of the railway station at Derbunga on the morning we left, the 20th of December, we were fortunate in getting a fine view of Mount Everest, 29,000 feet, the highest of the Himalayan range, 180 miles distant. Two grand snowy peaks were distinctly visible by the eye, and plainer still by the aid of a glass. The sky was cloudless.

On returning to the Ganges from Derbunga a branch of new railway was being laid at the river, where I observed that the carrying of earth was all done by women, in baskets on their heads, and coals were being landed on a wharf and carried by women in the same manner. On crossing the river we proceeded southwards by the East Indian Railway, through a country more or less rich. Towards nightfall we passed through Sonthal, where, some few years ago, the cultivators cut off the heads of some of their bankers, as the readiest way of paying their debts. It is a hilly and poorer country than most I have seen. In the morning we reached Burdwan, where at 6.30 we were received by the collector, and immediately driven some miles through a more fertile country to inspect its agriculture. The whole of this region within eighty miles of Calcutta is good rice land. There is generally rainfall sufficient to mature a rice crop, and year after year the same ground is called on for a new crop, which they say varies with the season, but on the whole shows no sign of exhaustion.

Walking through the rice fields, from which most of the crop is now cut, we come to a village among ponds of water. The mud huts have, in long generations of successive owners, gradually raised themselves above the dead level of the surrounding country—each new hut being founded on the ruins of those preceding it—at once raising the level of the dwellings, and sinking by the excavated soil the large and deep ponds which have yielded the material for the latest as well as the earliest erections. The villages are thus found to be situated on raised mounds, from which they overlook the subjacent rice plains; and, as it is only on these mounds that trees flourish in this wet country, each village has its fine ancestral trees overhanging the houses and shading the water. Among these are the two kinds of palm, the short but massive-leaved date palm, and the tall cocoa-nut palm overtopping all others. The people of Lower Bengal are a darker race than those in the north-west; they have jet-black hair, and many of the younger men go bareheaded in the sun. Having but one general crop, rice, they have vegetable gardens close to the villages, and these are certainly not less comfortable than those where greater variety of produce is raised. Every house has an outer house for the cattle, whence you enter a small court-yard, upon which the dwelling-house opens. Most of the buildings are of mud. Some are more substantial, and many of them with tile roofs, often covered with creepers, and bearing a fine crop of pumpkins, lying warm in the sun among their glistening leaves. The people seem to an English eye scantily clothed, but they have great freedom of movement; and as most of their body is covered with only its natural garment of dark shining skin, they are in no way dependent on the tailor for fashion, for theirs does not change. The women do not run off here at the sight of a stranger, and the men and boys readily enter into conversation. The dogs alone show a keen feeling of inhospitality, which their dark owners try in vain to dispel. The little oxen look shy, and the black buffalo cows must be very warily passed, as they lower their twisted horns with evident signs of sincerity.

This village is said to be a fair sample of those in the neighbourhood of Burdwan. The people are on the whole well-to-do. They have all good stocks of rice; some of them have four years' stores by them, stored in round stacks of unhusked rice. They spend so little; 7 lbs. of rice to a family of five will feed them handsomely—say 3½d. a day, or £5 6s. a year, and their clothing perhaps 30s. more. Nor do they desire to improve their mode of living. They drink no strong liquors, and the poorest of them are kind to poor relations. The Hindu religion enjoins this, and every one who has any land considers it a duty to feed the infirm and poor of his own kin. There is no poor-law, and until recent famine years there were no poor. If we compare with our agricultural labourers these people with their little farms, their cattle, and their rice, the Indian on this good soil has the better lot, so far as the enjoyment of life is concerned. He is his own master, works hard at seed-time and harvest, but has long spells of light or no work between. As prices rise, he will become independent of the Bunyia, and be able to treat with him on equal terms.

In Bengal there are three conditions only upon which the landowners can claim an advance of rent from cultivators who have permanent rights of occupancy: 1. If the land be found on measurement to be larger than was supposed. 2. If the land be held at a lower rent than the prevailing rate for similar land with equal advantages held by the same class of cultivators in the vicinity. 3. If the value of the produce, or the productive powers of the land, have increased otherwise than at the expense or by the agency of the cultivator. The court will grant a claim for abatement of the first and third in case the contrary may have occurred. The judge here is opposed to the extension of "occupancy rights," as certain to lead to more subdivision, because the Hindu law directs all property to be divided amongst sons. This has already, in some localities, led to the smallest subdivisions—a cowrie being in some instances the rent paid by an occupant, which indicates a density of population beyond the power of the soil to maintain it. The system of village communities is much safer, as it does not recognise individual rights of property, and thereby compels the superfluous population to go forth for the common safety. To limit the power of oppression by the Bunyia, it is recommended here to restore the old Hindu practice, that a debt should not be legally increased by interest to an amount beyond twice the original sum borrowed.

In the evening of Saturday we reached Calcutta, where we spent Sunday. I went to the cathedral, which is a handsome church, with a statue of Heber in the vestibule, and an inscription to the memory of my old school-fellow, Col. Robert Yule, who fell at the siege of Delhi, "bravest among the brave, and gentlest among the gentle." On the left of the door-way, there is a mural monument to Colonel Baird Smith, who directed the engineering operations which led to the capture of Delhi, and who died at the early age of forty-three, having, during his comparatively short career, rendered great services to India.

On Monday, the 23rd of December, we proceeded to Eastern Bengal, travelling through a very rich country, chiefly in rice, except where the land is slightly elevated above the flat plain, when it is covered with winter crops of wheat and barley, vegetables, mustard, and other luxuriant-growing oil plants. After travelling 180 miles through this richly cultivated country we reach Goalunda, the point of junction of the Ganges and Brahmapootra. These two grand rivers, starting from opposite sides of the same snowy range in the Himalayas—the one at first flowing west, and then, on reaching the plain, turning south-east; the other flowing east, and, after rounding the eastern end of the Himalayas, turning west—both, after a course of 1,000 miles, here mingle their waters, about 200 miles from the sea. They then become an immense river, far larger than the Mississippi at St. Louis. The Rhine and the Rhone are streamlets in comparison.

Here we embark in a two-funnelled steamer of great size, with comfortable little rooms on deck which we occupy for the next three nights, and in the usual bright sunshine we commence our cruise on this great inland navigation. You may go up the

Ganges seven hundred miles, up the Brahmapootra five hundred miles, up another river to Cachar two hundred miles, on all of which steamers ply, besides many smaller rivers and channels permeating the country, and covered with country boats bringing down jute to be shipped at Chittagong, 250 miles below us, for Dundee—or rice, and other produce with which this country teems, for Calcutta. The banks of the rivers are not above fifteen feet higher than the stream—rich alluvial mould. During the rains in June, July, and August, and, when the snow melts on the Himalayas, the greater part of the flat country becomes a sea, the rice and jute are covered with water, and the people in their villages, on the slightly elevated grounds, isolated, and communicating with each other by boats. This is not an unhealthy time. It is when the rains abate and the rivers return within their beds, and the soaked ground, covered with rank vegetation reeking in the blazing sun, throws out its exhalations, that fever sets in and carries off a large percentage of the population. This is not unfrequently followed by cholera, so that if nature has been prolific of soil and crop, it is not unattended with ills from which our more niggard soil and harsher climate are happily free. To the eye of the agriculturist the country at this season is magnificent. The people are all afoot, or in boats. As we open each new channel, fleets of white sails are coming down before a light breeze, graceful as swans; and at every village we pass—and they are thick along the banks—the people are laving water, bathing in the stream, or plying their little high-sterned boats nimbly about. Every mile or two we pass what appears like the spire of a village church, but which really marks the place where some Nawab's body was burned, the spiral form of monument being here used instead of the more common dome.

The valley of the Brahmapootra contains 20,000 square miles of fine alluvial land. This is more than double the area of the cultivated land of Egypt, all fertile, and much of it with abundance of fine coal, and an ample rainfall. It is traversed by a navigable river; but, with all these advantages, it is obliged to import rice for the support of the imported coolies who work the tea estates. There is every opportunity and motive for colonisation—people too numerous and on the edge of famine if the rains fail, within 600 or 800 miles, with railway most of the way, and a navigable river, and the same supreme Government; and yet three-fourths of this fertile region are still in jungle. In the Garrow Hills, which project into this plain, coal of excellent quality is found within 250 miles of Calcutta, with water carriage, wanting only a connecting link between the river and the coal field. Though surrounded by our stations, this high country is inhabited by lawless tribes, and is still marked in the maps as "unexplored."

The rivers are constantly encroaching in one place and leaving another. We passed two large castles, both of which were originally some miles away from the river, but from change of its course are now undermined and sliding into it, the roofs and all the woodwork having been removed. The river bank is lined for some miles with cottages made of bamboo, and covered with steep thatched roofs. The cultivators who inhabit them are ready to move back or forward as the river alters its course, fresh fields being at their disposal in exchange for those which the river absorbs. They are charged very low rates for this rich fresh alluvial land, a mere acknowledgment, as it is capable of growing any crop, but subject to this risk. The captain of the steamer, who has been many years on these rivers, tells me that three coolies will do as much work as one European, if employed by contract. There is much pottery made along the banks and shipped on the river. We passed a steamer with two large cargo boats tied to her side, carrying from 1,400 to 2,000 tons of produce. They gather this on the river side, some going to Goalundo, whence it passes by railway to Calcutta, some direct by water to Calcutta or to Chittagong. This part of the country has been greatly enriched by the extension of jute, the cultivators hitherto getting all the profit, as united action has enabled them to resist an increase of rent, and the value of the crop is three times greater than that of rice. This, by diminishing the area of rice, has lessened the supply of food more than is thought to be either safe or desirable. We land on the bank, and walk through the fields to a village which displays many signs of prosperity, in good houses, and plentiful reserves of grain stored up in large beehive-like stacks for future sale or consumption.

Turning up the branch river to Dacca, we meet numbers of cargo vessels coming down under full sail, and pass two sea-going ships at anchor and taking in cargo. The left bank has a continued succession of villages, nestling among the trees, and is very populous, some parts having 1,000 to the square mile. Small boats crowded with people are moving about, and the scene is lively and gay in the warm sunshine, the light but cooling breeze, and the sparkling water. We pass a white steamer, with a lighter covered with awnings tied to her side, in which the commissioner is making his rounds to his different stations. Then an indigo factory, no longer used, the cultivation of indigo having been given up here, the increasing value of other crops rendering it comparatively unremunerative. Some kinds of jute grow on dry land, some three feet deep in water. There is no artificial irrigation here, but the overflow of the Brahmapootra covers the country and leaves a rich deposit upon which jute and rice equally thrive. Two crops of rice in a year are quite common, one the wet, the other the dry crop, and as there is a fresh deposit with every annual flood the land improves under this system.

The land is held under permanent settlement, and as the Government has no immediate interest in the question of rent, the landlords and their tenants fight that out with the help of the courts of law, the tenants making up a common purse for the purpose. The law's delay, and the difficulty of dealing with large numbers of small tenants, enable these to get the upper hand by uniting against enhancement of rents, and even against any rent, as the landlord is called on by the courts to show by his books that he has received the precise rent for five years back; otherwise they will not grant him a decree, thus casting the onus on him to show that he is entitled to rent. A large landowner complained to me that while Government exacts its rent to the day, or sells the estate of the defaulter, its courts throw such difficulties in his way, that from three of his estates, with hundreds of small occupiers, he is unable to get any rent, as in each single case he is compelled to sue, and it has become a question whether it will pay to do so. The circumstances here are the reverse of what we found them in the North-West Provinces. There the Government interfered to protect the cultivator from the landlord by giving him "occupancy rights," which, being transferable, were quickly pawned by the poor man to the money-lender. Here the cultivators, being near good markets, have become so independent that the landlord asks for Government assistance against them. Their united action in withholding rent is a serious matter, especially to the small landowners, whose caste and condition often forbid them to cultivate the land themselves, and who are thus dependent on the rent for their living. The lesson to be drawn from these opposite results would seem to be that the less the Government, and the courts of law, interfere in the relations between landlord and tenant, the more likely are they to be satisfactorily arranged by the mutual interests of the parties.

I found the price of salt here three-halfpence a pound. A family of four will consume four pounds a month, or 48 lbs. in a year, at a cost of 6s. The duty is nine-tenths of the price, or in this case about 5s. 5d., and, as the earnings of the family are 16s. a month, the salt-tax costs them the thirty-fifth part of their wages. This is equal in our term to a sevenpenny income-tax, but it presses most heavily on the poorest, though it indeed is the only tax, direct or indirect, which the mass of the people pay.

The rivers here swarm with fish, which must be salted to preserve them for transport, but the cost of salt is three times that of the fish, and an abatement of the duty for fish-curing is allowed by Government.

Dacca is an ancient city standing on the edge of a navigable river, on an elevation of red clay some twenty feet higher than the low rice plain. It was before our time first a Portuguese, and then a French station, originally for the Dacca muslin trade, a manufacture which is still carried on. There is a military station which, at the Mutiny, was recaptured from the mutineers by the officers and sailors of the fleet. In the vicinity there is a fine park, with a good race-course, the sport on which is greatly enjoyed by the native population.

We were invited by the Nawab to a garden party on the river side, where there was a good instrumental band. He took us through his large and handsome house, and I had much useful conversation with him.

Some miles from the town, when driving into the country, we met a man carrying on his head a nicely balanced load of earthen pots, packed on a circular hoop crossed with string. It was balanced by a stick held over the shoulder keeping it all square. He had fifty of these pots, weighing together 120 lbs., on his head, and was stepping along at a quick springing trot, a capital mode of conveying brittle ware over a bad road. Other men were carrying equally neatly arranged head-loads of vegetables and fruit to the Dacca market. There is a large export of rice from this division, amounting last year to 150,000 tons.

In the district below Backergunge, which was swept a few years ago by the terrible storm waves, the land is so productive that the people who were left are quickly recovering prosperity. They are self-reliant and industrious, and live in great comfort, spending their money freely at the fairs in the idle season from January to May. They dwell in homesteads of two or three acres, with a raised road running to the river, lined on each side by cocoa-nut and date palms and other fruit trees. They have an outer house where they transact business, receive visitors, and put up guests for the night, and an inner house for the family. So productive is the soil that many support themselves from their homestead gardens, and have the crop of their farms for sale.

On our return to Calcutta I had an opportunity of seeing the city and its environs during the Christmas week, when I had the honour of being the guest of the Viceroy. The population within municipal limits is 430,000, of whom two-thirds are males, and one-third females. This remarkable disparity is shared in a less degree by the city of Bombay, but not at all by that of Madras, where the sexes are equal in number. The total population of each province shows no such disparity, Bengal and Madras having an equal proportion. The Hindus and Mohammedans are as two to one in the city of Calcutta, and province of Bengal.

The city stands on the Hooghly branch of the Ganges, about 80 miles from the sea, to which it is navigable by large ships. The river-bank of Calcutta is lined with shipping, from which, and from the fortress, a fine park stretches along the front of the city to the grounds of Government House, the residence of the Viceroy. This park, the Maidan, is very extensive, and includes a race-course, and abundant space for the exercise of troops and the recreation of the public. It contains numerous statues of personages more or less notable, and a lofty pillar, the most conspicuous object in Calcutta, to the memory of Sir David Ochterlony, "statesman and soldier," who died in 1825. Of Clive and Warren Hastings I found no memorial here. There are equestrian statues of Lord Hardinge and Lord Mayo, with appropriate inscriptions, and "to Earl Canning, Governor-General, and first Viceroy of India," with the date of his birth and death, but nothing more. Remembering the trying times of the Mutiny, and the calm courage he displayed during those terrible months, it struck me that the words, *mens æqua in arduis,* would be an appropriate addition. In the neighbourhood is a statue of the great Governor-General, Lord Lawrence. In the beautiful public gardens nearest to the shipping stands in white marble the statue of "Sir William Peel, V.C., K.C.B., commander of the Naval Brigade in the War of the Indian Mutiny," whose ship-guns I saw at Lucknow, and whose courage and devotion, and too early death, will not soon be forgotten by his countrymen. At Calcutta, as at previous halting-places, the Famine Commission held careful courts of inquiry, having here an opportunity of examining several of the higher officials who had had practical experience of the management of Indian famines.

CHAPTER VIII.

MADRAS.—TRICHINOPOLY.—MADURA.

We left Calcutta on the 2nd of January at 7 a.m., and spent all the day going down the river to the Sandheads, in the troopship "Tenasserim," in which we were so fortunate as to get a passage to Madras. The low banks of the river are much wooded, the palm being predominant. Towards evening we passed the revolving light, and soon afterwards stood on a south-west course across the "black water." The evening was very fine with clear moonlight, the stars glancing bright from the dark background through light fleecy clouds. The next morning brought a fine breeze, brightening the colour of the translucent water, now, under the influence of powerful sunlight, a sparkling blue. We pass Juggernaut, which stands on the edge of the sea. Next day we are off Vizigapatam, having passed Ganjam in the night. The line of coast is partly low, and partly long hills with peaks in the distance rising from 600 up to 2,000 feet. The town lies at the foot of the hills, a temple, prominently placed on a spur, overlooking the harbour. In that part are the places of business, and, to the east of it, the native town of thatched mud-houses. About a mile farther the villa suburb, where the houses of the principal inhabitants are built, stands on a low height amidst evergreens and trees, open to the refreshing sea breeze, and, as seen from the sea, very like the villas on the road from Cannes to Nice.

Boats of the most primitive build come off with oysters, vegetables, and poultry. They are simply three pieces of timber, about nine inches square and twelve feet long, tied together at each end, and pointed to pierce the wave. Two men kneeling, the one in the front, the other in the stern, propel them by a small oar or paddle, the wave running in over the bows and out at the stern. The harbour master came off in a large Mussowlie boat which carries many people, the rowers keeping time by a monotonous chant. These boats have their planks bound together by cord, not by nails, and are so elastic that the planks do not break, but "give," when the boat is driven broadside on the beach by the heavy surf which nearly always runs upon this coast. We landed through a great wave over the bar, but without surf, inside a quiet harbour, shut in by rounded hills, not unlike Dartmouth. It was the last day of the feast of Mohurrum, and the whole population were in the streets in gala suit, following processions of fragile but showy erections with figures carried on platforms shoulder high by men with painted faces, preceded by drums. The people looked well fed and clad, and all were gay and in high spirits, much like a country fair at home. There was quite a brilliant display of colour, the women and girls with jewels, or gold or silver ornaments in their noses, and on their arms and ankles.

The system of land tenure here is that of large landowners, a few small ones, and the remainder cultivators. The rent paid by the last is about three times that which the Government receives from the landowners. The cultivators seldom have rights of occupancy, but they are not oppressed by the zemindars. The labourers without land are worst off, as there is little demand for labour. The Collector's district here is 21,000 square miles, and is larger and more populous than Greece or Denmark.

We returned to the ship in the evening. Already we feel the increasing heat of a more southerly clime. Though careering over the waves, with a strong breeze, we sleep with cabin windows wide open. There is always bright sunshine by day, and brilliant starlit skies by night. But, lovely though it is at sea, the hard light and glare on shore make one long for the veiled sunshine of an English morning.

Next morning we were off Coconada, the sea-port of the navigable canals and great irrigation works of the Godavery. These works, which are a monument of the engineering skill and ability of Sir Arthur Cotton, are confined to the delta of that river. It has a course of 900 miles, and receives various affluents—making with it a total mileage of 2,610—420 miles of which are capable of navigation, above the Anicut, for five months of the year. On the main river the general fall does not exceed one foot in the mile. Below the gorge where the river breaks through the eastern Ghâts, navigation is practicable most part of the year. In this gorge the river is narrowed from a width in some places of two miles to 300 yards, the hills rising from the water's edge to a height of more than 2,000 feet. Here the scenery is very fine, and has been compared to that of the Rhine. Emerging from the gorge which it has traversed for twenty miles, the river spreads itself into a broad stream, dotted with islands, till passing out of the hills it continues its course to the great Anicut of Dowlaisherum, whence it is conducted through the fertilised delta by a network of irrigation canals to its outlets at the sea. These canals are constructed for navigation also, so that they serve the double purpose of producing a crop, and of conveying it to market.

The area of delta land irrigated by the Godavery is 540,000 acres. The soil is a black deposit, carried down by the river, and gradually spread over its sandy delta. The crop chiefly grown is rice. In the famine year of 1876—7, rice to the value of half a million sterling was exported from Coconada. There is seldom more than one crop of rice taken the same year, either because there is not time for a second crop to mature, or because the first crop exhausts the land so much that it cannot yield a second until it has had a fresh coat from the irrigation of the wet season. The cost to the Government of interest and maintenance is about 1s. 8d. an acre, and as the rates paid by the cultivator are 16s. an acre for a sugar crop, 8s. for rice, 4s. for dry crop, there is a very large profit to Government from the Godavery irrigation. The exports of produce from Coconada have increased eightfold in consequence of the irrigation works, and each five years continues to show a growing increase. The canals of the Kistna, which are now connected by the Buckingham Canal with the Godavery, afford irrigation to 265,000 acres, and both systems are capable of considerable extension, and, from the few locks and bridges required, are peculiarly favourable for navigation also. The Buckingham Canal, completed during the late famine, affords a boat communication of 400 miles between these districts and Madras.

Landing at Madras, we disembarked from the Mussowlie boat at the central jetty, thus escaping the surf on the beach. Considerable progress has been made in the erection of the concrete piers now advancing from the shore at each extremity of the new harbour works. Unlike those of Alexandria and Port Said, the quays are built with a perfectly smooth face, the force of the wave here being greater, and this mode of construction being for that reason preferred by the engineer, who entertains the fullest confidence in the future success of the harbour works, not as yet, however, realised. The inconvenience of the surf which constantly runs along this open shore is not, except in gales at the time of the monsoon, a serious obstacle to trade. During the late famine there was more work done in landing cargo than the most sanguine ever expect to see as a regular trade, and it was all done by lighters, loading and unloading from the ships at anchor in the offing. All along this coast, notwithstanding the surf-wave, the same safety in landing cargo by Mussowlie boats can be counted on.

Approaching it from the sea, Madras is seen to advantage. There is a long flat coast clothed with trees, among which, in openings of the woods, portions of the city become visible. The tower of the lighthouse, the large white house the residence of the Governor, with its park, next to it the fort, and then the handsome new buildings of the Legislative Assembly and the Revenue Board, come prominently into view. The temperature is at this season, January, eight degrees higher than that of Calcutta, but the fine sea breeze compensates for that. Though the climate is more damp and unpleasant, it is not unhealthy, and the city is well supplied with water. It is 840 miles from Calcutta by sea, and ten degrees nearer the equator. In a population of about 400,000, there is a larger proportion of Christians, and a smaller of Mohammedans, than in any of the other great cities of India, three-fourths of the people being Hindus, one-eighth Mohammedans, one-eleventh Christians, and the remainder various.

The country is well clothed with wood, and, except in the thickly populated parts of the town, the houses of the poorer class are embowered in shrubberies, and those of the Europeans placed in handsome, park-like enclosures. There are fine roads in all directions, and large sweeps of lake-like rivers and canals. The military bands play on alternate evenings at the seaside in the cooling breeze, within sound of the heavy booming wave that never ceases to break on this open shore. This may be termed "the Row" of Madras, whence the carriages convey their owners to the Club, where the ladies interview each other, while the gentlemen go in to learn the latest news before returning home with them to dinner.

In extent and population the Presidency of Madras exceeds by a little that of the United Kingdom. The food crops cover an area nearly twice as great as ours, 22,500,000 acres compared with 11,600,000. One-fifth of the whole is irrigated land, but not quite one-third of that derives its supply from unfailing sources, the rivers which take their rise in the western range of mountains, and are fed by the monsoon rains. The remainder is dependent on reservoirs or tanks, which collect the rainfall in the low country, are generally shallow basins, which, when full, cover as much land as they serve, and are liable to be rapidly evaporated by the scorching heat of the sun. The proportion of level land is much less than that of Bengal or the North-West Provinces, and, except in the alluvial plains of the great rivers, the soil is poorer in quality, and, under the present exhaustive system, rapidly deteriorating in productiveness.

One fourth of the Presidency is under zemindars who have a "permanent settlement," the majority of whom are said not to be good landlords. Three-fourths are under the ryotwary system, the cultivators holding their lands directly from the Crown. Among these there is little or no litigation about land, the practice being to give any unoccupied land to the first applicant. The result of the two systems appears to be much the same when viewed in contiguous tracts, the tenant of the zemindar who pays a higher rent than the Government ryot showing no outward sign, either in his cultivation, his house, or mode of living, that would indicate any inferiority in his condition; the ryot's power of minute subdivision amongst his sons constantly tending in both cases towards poverty. The ryot's rights are heritable and transferable, and are very valuable on the rich well-watered land. On the poorer soils they are of little value, and are often resigned to the Government.

There are twenty collectorates in the Presidency, on seven or eight of which a settlement of the land revenue for thirty years has been completed, which has resulted in a considerable increase, chiefly from the discovery of land that had escaped assessment. The test of increase, however, is not the productive power of the land, but the rise of prices as affected by situation, and the opening of railways or roads to better markets. The collectorates are generally too large in extent, many collectors having, with three European assistants, to superintend districts as large and populous as Belgium. The tendency here of officialism is to bring every person into subjection to the rule of the leading officials in the capital, who are constantly asking for returns and statistics, which, though often laid aside and buried in their bureaus when they get them, occupy much of the time of the district officers in inquiry and preparation. The natural relations between landlord and tenant are occasionally made the subject of experimental theories by men who never had any land of their own, but, when placed in power, desire to leave their mark on this great social question.

Within easy reach of the city of Madras is the experimental farm of Sydapet, under the very able management of Mr. Robertson. Many experiments of great interest to Indian agriculturists are being carried out here, both in the cultivation and management of crops, and in the improvement of the breed of live stock. The economical application of water to the growing crops, in a country where water is so essential, has been carefully studied, and the sandy porous soil of this farm makes the study a matter of supreme necessity. The rainfall supplies one-third, and irrigation two-thirds, of the 5,400 tons of water which each acre of the soil of this farm requires for the production of a good crop. A well with a double lift, worked by one bullock, yields 100 tons, or one inch of water over an acre, in a day. By the machinery here adopted one bullock does nearly the usual work of two. The application of water in ordinary seasons doubles the crop where the ground is manured, and in seasons of drought makes a crop certain. But the cost of its application from a well, if all labour is counted, is not less than 40s. to 50s. an acre. Where water is got by gravitation from a canal, there is generally great waste of this expensive but valuable article. One of the points most insisted upon as the result of Mr. Robertson's experience here is the necessity in India of economising water for irrigation. The next is the substitution of wood fuel for cow-dung in order to preserve the manure for the land. This, he finds, might be done by planting hedge-row timber, the *Inga dulcis*, of quick growth, which after three years would yield four tons of wood fuel per mile. The manure itself might be largely increased by fodder crops: cholum, if irrigated, will yield five crops in a season. This, he thinks, might be grown on part of the fallows, of which in Madras there are four million acres. Guinea grass is found a capital rotation crop for grazing, as it cleans and refreshes the land when put down for two years. The area of wheat in Madras is small, the temperature being too high for it.

The improvement in the breed of sheep has been attempted here by selection, and crossing native breeds. The merino cross will be tried. The produce of the breed when improved is distributed over the country for the same purpose through the civil officers.

As an educational establishment Sydapet has sixty students of the average age of twenty-two, who have previously matriculated at the universities. They are Parsees and Brahmins and others, from Bombay and Madras, who will return to their own districts as instructors in agriculture. They go through a regular three years' course of chemistry, botany, zoology, veterinary surgery, surveying, and bookkeeping, and are employed an hour in the field every morning in practical agriculture. The students are thus not only instructed in the several sciences connected with agriculture, but are familiarised with its practice, and with the instructive experiments in the use of water and manure, the improvement in the breeds of live stock, and the economy of labour by improved implements and machinery.

One of the most interesting experiments which has been made at Sydapet is that of the value of cow-dung as manure in its natural state, compared with the ashes of the same quantity after being burnt and used as fuel. The former weighed 3,150 pounds, the latter 130 pounds. To two equal adjoining plots of land these severally were applied, and a third plot had no manure. The plots were otherwise treated alike, and the whole was sown with a green fodder crop of cholum. The weight of fodder from the first and second cuttings was:—

	Plot 1, with manure	Plot 2, with ashes of manure	Plot 3, nothing.
	lbs.	lbs.	lbs.
First cutting . . .	4,058	4,368	3,140
Second cutting . . .	1,680	1,176	896
Weight of both Cuttings	5,738	5,544	4,036

The ashes thus gave the largest crop at the first cutting, the manure in that form more quickly yielding its strength. At the second cutting, the more slowly acting dung showed the larger result. But the weight of the two cuttings together is so nearly alike as to lead to the inference that the universal practice in India of using the dung first for fuel, and afterwards as ashes for manure, ought not to be too hastily condemned. This being a question of great economical importance, I ventured to press on Mr. Robertson the propriety of repeating and testing the experiment. Very great advantage to India is likely to result from the well-considered experiments carried on here by Mr. Robertson.

The Governor, the Duke of Buckingham, took me out with him to the country to an afternoon party, five miles from town. It was a charming afternoon, with a fine breeze from the sea, and we drove over a good road through quite a park-like English country. The house, that of Mr. Justice Kearnan, is finely situated on a river, in the midst of grounds and gardens plentifully interspersed with flowers and flowering trees. There was a large and pleasant party, and a kind and hospitable host.

After taking the evidence, for several consecutive days, of the leading officials, including that of the Duke of Buckingham, the Governor, we left Madras on the evening of the 16th of January, to visit the southern part of the Presidency. At six next morning we were at Erode in the valley of the Cauvery, described by the Duke of Wellington, in 1804, in words exactly applicable to its present condition. "Innumerable canals," he says, "are cut from it, from its rise in the western mountains till it falls into the sea. And these happy countries are certain of a crop, whether rains are abundant or otherwise. No river in India is so much taken advantage of, and none with such a fall, and banks so low, and therefore naturally so capable of use." From Erode to Trichinopoly the railway skirts this plain, along which the main canal is carried, whence the water is carefully spread over the richer ground on the flat, and thence to the little squares that divide each owner's patch. Here rice is most carefully planted and cultivated, and is seen in all stages of growth. Nothing can exceed the perfection of this rice culture. Every plant has its place, and not a blank is visible.

From the top of the rock of Trichinopoly, which rises 400 feet out of the plain, it was extremely pleasant to breathe the invigorating air, and enjoy the lovely view in the setting sun. As far as the eye could reach the rich plain, watered by the canals, was covered with vegetation. The Cauvery, with its affluents, waters probably a greater area than any river in India. Besides the irrigation of its valley in Mysore, and its further course through the districts of Coimbatore, Salem, and Trichinopoly, the irrigated area of Tanjore alone is 725,000 acres. Its revenue exceeds that of any other river in India, and nowhere has the cost of construction and maintenance been on so moderate a scale. The system of irrigation here is very ancient, and the Cauvery has been preserved from the danger of its waters passing into the Coleroon, by Sir Arthur Cotton's great work in 1836, the Anicut, which controls the river at the head of the delta, and enables the engineer to direct its course at his discretion. The range of the Shevaroy hills bounds and is seen along the northern edge of the plain, one hill of which very much resembles Arthur's Seat at Edinburgh.

The villages are built of the red clay of the country; the houses thatched, small, and poor. There are no gardens round the villages, and the people are much alike everywhere. Here is a man sitting on his haunches with a large bundle tied up in a white cloth beside him, and but for the man's head it would be difficult to tell which is the man and which the bundle. We pass small temples, with figures of horses on each side, looking towards them. The great Hindu temple of Trichinopoly, with its 1,000 pillars, and 10,000 people living within its external walls, appeared to me grotesque, extravagant, and anything but awe-inspiring. Not a feeling of reverence entered my mind as I walked through the tawdry aisles, and no room was found for it when, at the most sacred spot, where the jewels of the idols were brought out for exhibition, a Nautch girl began her dance to a monotonous jig tune, and a couple of elephants, taught by their keepers to make a begging snort, at the same time appealed to our sympathy. The temple is built on an island among the devious waters of the river, and approached by a bridge through groves of palms, and other lofty trees, which hide its great extent.

The collectorate of Trichinopoly was re-settled for thirty years in 1864. It contains 356 villages, and the Government assessment was then reduced 25 per cent. Since the time when Clive lived here, in a house still standing at the foot of the Rock, and from times much more recent, population has largely increased. Prices have risen, railways have been made, export markets have been opened up, irrigation has been improved, life and property are secure—but the land revenue declines! And for the plain reason, that no limit is placed to the subdivision of property, and thereby every encouragement is given to the increase of population. By the Hindu law of subdivision among male children, an estate of 100 acrès held by one man may be reduced in three generations to holdings of three-fourths of an acre each. And many are in that condition, for the majority will stay at home, and subdivision becomes excessive.

The Government charge for land in river-irrigated villages here is not one-third of what is paid in some other localities no better in quality. It is not the productive quality of the soil that must alone be considered by a paternal Government which is also the landowner, but the capacity it possesses to maintain the population upon it. In a generation or two more, if this principle of subdivision remains unchecked, there will be no revenue left to the Government. Even the rich soil of Tanjore, with a population now exceeding 1,000 per square mile, is said to be noticeably falling off in productiveness.

In the native states along the coast of Western India, from Cape Comorin to Goa, there has been for many centuries a system of strict entail, by which the eldest son succeeds to all the property, and the rest of the sons are not allowed to marry. Large estates have thus during all that period been kept together. The cultivators have leases for twelve years, with a renewal fine every twelfth year. A sum of money is paid at the beginning, and the use of the land is given as interest on this sum; but the fine was originally stipulated for, and the connection is thus maintained for generations. The cultivators may subdivide, but there are as many adding to their lands as those who diminish them, and the proportion of small properties does not increase.

Sugar-cane, plantain, saffron, betel, are all grown in the Trichinopoly district, and yield good returns. There is also some black soil suitable for cotton, which, however, is not much grown. The ashes of cow-dung are carefully preserved for manure, but town refuse is little prized.

Crossing the ridge of dry land towards Madura, we go through a country which was heavily pressed by the famine—a red stony soil, dry and parched, most of it lying uncultivated, and all showing signs of deficient water supply, and unremunerative agriculture. Within a few miles of Madura, we pass into the valley of the Vigay, where the cultivation improves greatly, the supply of water being there tolerably certain. At Madura we are within ten degrees of the equator, and the sun is very powerful.

The early morning is the best time for exploring this ancient city of 52,000 people. The palace of the kings is unroofed, some two and a half centuries old, but very spacious and magnificent. It was a real pleasure to wander through the grand colonnades, which are now being restored to be used for the courts of law, compared with the tawdry and grotesque ornaments of the famous Hindu pagodas in the immediate vicinity. The high towers of the latter are, however, wonderful in their way in point of construction and ornament.

Madura is a great centre of Christian missionary enterprise—English, American, and German—all of whom claim a large measure of success here. It is gained primarily through schools at which orphan children are brought up and educated, and through the native women teachers, who are readily admitted to the zenanas. The Hindu here is said to be a difficult subject to work upon, patient and dumb in politics and therefore easily ruled, but tyrannical over his women—timid, selfish, and often untruthful. His best quality is his appreciation of, and implicit trust in, the justice of the British officers. The American missionary told me this was a genuine feeling of the people, who, though very poor, are better off than when he first came to the country thirty years ago. Many go to Ceylon to earn wages at the coffee and other plantations there, in order to return and buy land, their highest earthly ambition being the possession of a piece of land in their native villages. To convert them into labourers would, he thinks, be to bring them entirely under the power of their native employer, who is seldom liberal or just.

Returning by the same route to Erode, we traverse a very well-cultivated country, though narrowed by the highlands on each side, to Coimbatore. It produces sugar, tobacco, chilies, and grain crops. The water is got from wells at a depth of twenty to thirty feet. Of the eighty thousand landholders in the district, fifty thousand pay less than 20s. each of annual rent. There is great competition for the purchase of land which has right of water for irrigation, £80 to £100 an acre being paid for it. Dry land with no right of water brings about as many shillings. The habits of the cultivating class are said to be very brutish and immoral in this part of the country. From Coimbatore to the foot of the Nilghiries the land is very fine.

CHAPTER IX.

OOTACAMUND.—THE WYNAAD.—MYSORE.

At Metapollium, we leave the plain to enter upon an ascent of 8,000 feet, which is accomplished in a tonga, or two-wheeled dog-cart, drawn by two horses, from a pole fastened to either saddle, curricle fashion. The splendid mountain in front of us without a cloud to its summit, and clothed with wood up all its grand gorges, with little waterfalls glistening through the green precipices, and interspersed with masses of feathery bamboos gracefully intercepting the brilliancy of the sun, and with crimson flowers of the wild rhododendron, and brightly coloured creepers of every hue, was a sight never to be forgotten. We zigzagged for hours, each change of horses taking us 1,500 feet up, till the coffee plantations, at an elevation of 4,000 feet, are reached, which increase in extent till they cover the mountain-side up to 6,000 feet—very steep, but very regular and tidy, the smooth green bushes in rows like dwarfed bays. The manager's house, the packing houses, and the coolie lines, all betoken the presence of arrangement and capital, and form a marked contrast to the squalid native villages of the rich plain below. At a still higher elevation we see handsome single villas, nestling among green tree-covered rocky terraces, and finally reach the summit of the gorge at the Wellington Barracks, used for convalescent soldiers sent here from the low country, where many poor fellows find a last resting-place in the pretty cemetery at the riverside. Here we enter upon an elevated open country, like Exmoor or the Cheviots, without trees or bushes; after passing through which for some ten miles farther, we drop down upon the wood-clothed Ootacamund, the hill station and seat of Government of Madras during the hot weather, and then the fashionable resort of that Presidency. It is extremely pretty—villas on hill-tops surrounded by trees, not unlike those on the common at Tunbridge Wells, and now, in the middle of January, with weather like a cool, pleasant, sunny summer day at home. There are public gardens, and a pretty lake fills up the winding hollow, with a drive of some three or four miles round it. In this pleasant spot we spent some days examining commissioners, collectors, planters, and gold-miners, and in walking and riding over the neighbouring country.

We rode through the Government chinchona plantation here, for the production of the febrifuge, quinine, which is extracted from the bark of the tree. The bark is cut from the growing tree in alternate strips running up the tree, leaving an interval between the strips to be taken the next year, and resting it the third. The naked strip is covered with moss bound round the tree, and, underneath the moss, a new skin or bark forms. The plantation is carefully managed, and in suitable situations the chinchona is found more profitable than either coffee or tea. The elevation here is 6,000 to 6,500 feet, and the exposure north-east, so that no injury should be done to the trees by the south-west monsoon. Eight years are necessary in the growth of the young tree before the bark is sufficiently matured to bear its subsequent treatment. In the tenth year the return may be 400 lbs. of dry bark per acre, and about 450 trees per acre come to maturity. The plantation costs £80 an acre to bring into bearing. Two coolies an acre receive constant employment. The gathering of the crop, delivery in London, and the collecting of the moss cost £6 an acre. When well managed, and at present prices (12s. a pound), it is highly remunerative. There is room for its extension, but officialism, here as in other parts of India, is said not to favour the introduction of European capital, and is against the creation in India of wage-paying classes. The assessment or rent charged by the Government for land occupied by Europeans, as quoted to me here, is almost double that charged to native cultivators.

Coffee plantations are fairly successful on the sides of the plateau, but not higher. Tea is not so likely to pay, for the south-west monsoon, instead of bringing the warm rain which develops the leaf, is cold and ungenial. This might in some degree be ameliorated by planting the elevated ridges for shelter, as is said to be done with much advantage in Ceylon, where 100 yards in width is reserved along all ridges for a belt of shelter timber. The wattle-tree, the bark of which is much valued for tanning in Australia, has been introduced, and is expected to be capable of profitable extension here.

The Wynaad gold-field is in this part of the country. The Government geologist, Mr. Brough Smythe, who (in addition to official men and planters) was examined by us, and has had much experience in the Australian gold-fields, considers this to be as fine a field of quartz-bearing gold as he has seen. But it is not of the alluvial kind which attracts the digger with no other capital than his pick, and therefore there is no chance of a labourers' rush to these diggings. It is gold in the quartz veins of the solid rock, that requires machinery and considerable capital to extract, and still greater skill to be released from the pyrites with which it is conjoined. These gold-beds have been more or less worked for many generations, and there is some hope that the improved machinery of the present day may ere long render them more productive than at any former period. Ancient workings of a scientific character, far beyond the present skill of the natives, have been recently discovered.

The people who do not change are the peasants. They produce from the ground the means of living with the smallest amount of labour; they increase and multiply in prosperous years, and when famine comes they are swept off in thousands, and reduced to the standard of ordinary food production. There is, however, one aboriginal race, called the "Todas," in these highlands, which is said to be rapidly dying out. They make a precarious existence by their flocks, and live apart from other races. The Government maintains "reserves" for them. They are to some extent nomadic, moving about as they list for the convenience of their sheep and goats—a dirty, black, long-haired people, repulsive in appearance, and abject in manner. They differ from the Hindus in this, that instead of the men having more than one wife, the women have a variety of husbands.

The Hindu woman may well complain of subjection: she walks behind her husband, does not sit in his presence, eats humbly of the victuals he leaves, and addresses him as lord. A wife, if asked to tell her husband's name, puts her hand over her mouth, and refuses to do so as wanting in respect to him. The women do most of the work out of doors. They carry on their heads the heavy burdens, weed the crops, help to cut them, and do the grinding of the corn, the cooking of the meals, and into the long hours of the night weave the clothes. The men confine their labour chiefly to the working of the bullocks, and all thereto pertaining. Bullocks do all the farm work and all the cartage. There is not a cart-horse in India.

On returning from the hills to the plain, I had some conversation with the horse proprietor who posts this road. The famine had been very bad in the plain, and there was a constant flow of people up to the hills in the hope of finding something better. But as there was nothing to be got there, it was found necessary to station the police at the head of the Ghat, to turn them back, and hundreds then died in the woods or on the roads. At Metapollium, on the plain, the scenes of want and famine were dreadful, the starving people following the post-horses to pick up, and ravenously devour, any undigested corn dropped by the horses. And yet how soon do all traces of the famine disappear after the surplus have died! Along this road, as we passed, a tramway was being constructed, on which men, women, and boys were all engaged, and all were active, well fed, and cheerful. Even children, who are the first to fail in famine, seemed swarming in the villages.

Our next halt was at Bangalore, in the native State of Mysore, where we were most hospitably received by the Resident, Mr. Gordon. It is a plateau 2,000 feet higher than the plain, and the night temperature is sensibly colder; but even at this season, the 25th of January, there are musquitoes. The roses here are very fine, and the first I have seen in India, and they, with mignonette and heliotrope, give colour and perfume to the rooms. The young Maharajah will be of age in two years, when he will assume the authority now exercised by the Resident. The famine struck this

State with terrible severity; about one-seventh of the people died. The city contains a population of 142,000. In the fort is the cell where Sir David Baird was chained to a native prisoner.

There are handsome public and botanical gardens, and an experimental farm near the city. The manager of the latter, Mr. Harman, contends, from the experience he has had of the climate and soil, that if the land were deeply ploughed, and the cattle manure, instead of being used as fuel, applied direct to it, it would generally yield crops without artificial irrigation. Three crops may be taken in a year where there is "well" irrigation: first, maize, a three months' crop, used green as fodder; secondly, sweet potatoes; and thirdly, cholum or large millet. Captain Kensington, R.E., mentioned heavy crops grown by him experimentally, under native management, on good deep red soil, but not deep cultivation. The maximum produce on manured land was 2,650 lbs. of grain, and on land without manure, but with two years' fallow, 2,380 lbs. per acre. Potatoes from 98 lbs. of seed per acre gave a return of 9,800 lbs., on land watered from wells and manured. Two crops of potatoes can be grown in a year, and a crop of three months' maize between. Of eight hundred square miles surveyed by Captain Kensington, sixty are under "wet" cultivation, sixty are submerged by tanks for irrigation, two hundred and thirty are "dry" cultivation, and four hundred and fifty are waste but part cultivable. The gross produce per acre of the "dry" land is reckoned worth 40s., and is charged 2s. for Government rent; that of the "wet" land is worth 120s., and is charged 6s. for rent, the revenue taken by Government being in each case one-twentieth of the gross produce. This seemingly fair but erroneous principle leaves 38s. an acre in the hands of the one farmer, and 114s. to the other!

Descending 1,300 feet very gradually in about 100 miles to Jollarpet, we pass from a stony country into the rich plain which for ages has received the washings of the higher land. The palm is now again common, and the general appearance of the country is much richer than Mysore. As we proceed, the Penar valley is narrowed by projecting rocky hills till we pass from it into that of the Palar, where it widens into far reaches of fertile land, mostly under rice in all stages of growth—some just planted, some pushing through the glistening water, some coming into ear, and some under the sickle. The fields are small, and as these various processes are going on in the warm sunlight, the people are all out, and look picturesque in their divers-coloured garments—some planting, some reaping, others on the threshing-floor with the oxen treading out the corn, and here and there a shepherd and his boy leading and following their flock. The ground nut, which yields oil, and is largely exported, is being dug out and gathered, a numerous party working at this in line, under the superintendence of the cultivator. Women and children are all busy. Though the famine was very severe in some parts of this district, and the mortality great, there is no sign of want of labour either of man or beast, and the people look happy and in good condition. It is marvellous how quickly, in this country, the effects of famine are effaced, there being more room for those who survive it.

At Vellore, eighty miles from Madras, we lodged in the fort, a strong place in former times, surrounded by a ditch, the walls built of large granite blocks, but now commanded by high hills which are within range of modern artillery. Within its walls are a fine Hindu temple and a Mohammedan mosque, the former now used as a military post, the latter as a post-office. George the Fourth sent out a frigate to bring home the temple in pieces, to be set up at the Brighton Pavilion as a specimen of Hindu architecture. But war had meantime broken out, in which the frigate was employed for the transport of troops, and before it was concluded the king was gathered to his fathers, and his successor, King William, did not persevere with the project.

I visited the gaol, which is under the management of Major M'Leod. There were 1,540 prisoners inside, and 500 outside, under guard. The number increased one-fourth during the famine, dacoity (robbery by bands of more than five) being the principal crime. There is a central office, the roof of which overlooks the entire premises, on which a sentinel is always posted. From this centre eight separate compartments radiate, each with sleeping range in centre, and working sheds on each outer wall. The prisoners are divided equally amongst these; all are kept employed, the task being moderate, but each prisoner being capable of earning good marks entitling him, with good conduct, to more or less remission of sentence. Some make men's slippers and shoes, some do carpentry work, most weave handsome Indian carpets, the best of which are sent home to London for sale. The prisoners' clothing, and that of the police, are woven in the gaol. The prisoners have a bath every day when work is done; their condition and health are excellent, the death-rate last year being only one per cent. New-comers are manacled for the first three months. Incorrigible idlers are forced to carry weights round a circle at a good pace. The food is given in equal portions at ten and in the afternoon. On three days of the week each prisoner gets five ounces of mutton in addition to the daily meal of grain seasoned with salt and curry-powder, and a due proportion of vegetables. The average cost of food is £6 6s. a year. Every arrangement seemed good, and everything was most fresh, cleanly, and orderly, and in the highest degree creditable to the management.

In the evening we came on to Madras, where, as at all the principal stations, the Commission took lengthened evidence on famine management. Before leaving Madras I spent a night in his observatory with Mr. Pogson, the well-known astronomer, who has contributed valuable observations on the sun-spots as indicative of seasons of drought. These lead him to the conclusion that this Presidency is safe from famine, from that cause, for the next seven or eight years at least. The periodicity of droughts of great intensity seems pretty well established, but not their exact year or precise locality.

On the 1st of February we reached Cuddapah, 160 miles north of Madras, where the famine had been very severe. It is a cluster of villages in a rich plain, with fine mango and other trees shading the roads, bordered by a range of hills very bare but not high enough to afford a sanatorium. The place has a bad reputation for fever, but is in a rich, fertile country. From the rice-fields a heavy crop had just been reaped; and though (probably indeed because) in some parts of the district one-fourth of the people died during the late famine, all now look well fed and happy, and their cattle in fine condition.

After taking evidence from Europeans and natives in regard to the famine, we visited the canal of the Madras Irrigation Company, the lower division of a great project of Sir Arthur Cotton, which was originally meant to comprise two divisions. One of them was to carry the superfluous water of the Tungabhadra through the dry district of Bellary to the Kistna near Kurnool; another to take off a portion of the joint rivers Kistna and Tungabhadra near Kurnool, across the watershed separating it from the Pennair, the united waters then being turned into a canal where a navigable connection was ultimately to be formed with Nellore and the sea. A great area of land was thus to be irrigated, while the produce, for 400 miles, would have an outlet to the sea-coast. The lower half of the project has alone been constructed, that from Kurnool to Cuddapah, and as yet it has disappointed all expectation. An English company was formed, with authority to raise a capital of £1,000,000 on a Government guarantee of five per cent. But the cost of construction, based on estimates for deltaic districts, was enormously increased by the difficulty of crossing a rugged country, and the estimated capital was found quite inadequate to complete the work. Further sums were raised, and the guarantee extended, but an unexpected difficulty arose, in the refusal of the water by the cultivators of the black cotton soil, of which one-half at least of the irrigable land consists. The difficulties financially are thus doubled: first, by the vastly increased cost of the works beyond the original estimate; and secondly, by the want of demand for the water on so large a proportion of the irrigable area. Nor is the latter difficulty likely to be overcome, for in years of average rainfall the black fertile soils yield large crops without irrigation, their power of absorbing moisture from the atmosphere, and of retaining it, having been shown by the experiments at Sydapet to be six or eight times that of an ordinary dry soil. In a financial view this canal is a complete failure. The great value of wells, however, for irrigation was most forcibly shown in this district by the experience of the collector, Mr. Gribble, during the late famine.

North of Cuddapah we pass through a fertile, highly cultivated rice district, where the people were reaping and threshing heavy crops. We skirted several villages nestling among trees, and surrounded by good crops, a land of very small farms which in good years maintains, in abundance of rude food, a numerous population, who unfortunately have little thrift, or saving, to protect themselves in years of scarcity. All the really good land is occupied.

At Yarragoontha we enter the black soil where cholum, followed by cotton or indigo, is the usual succession, and where the larger fields of the same kind of crop indicate large holdings. The soil is underlaid by horizontal rock, which splits into thick slabs like Caithness flags, and affords excellent material for the numerous bridges which carry the railway over the wide but, at this season, dry beds of the rivers. The native Tahsildar of the district travelled part of the way with us: a very intelligent, observant man. Two-thirds of the ryots, or small landholders, he said, are poor, most of them as poor as the coolies who have no land. Five acres of the good black soil he reckons the minimum that a family can live comfortably upon, and ten acres of land of an inferior quality. The high prices have enriched the wealthier cultivators, but have impoverished the poorer. The increase of population, none of whom will leave their villages if they can eke out the scanty supply of food by nuts and seeds from the woods and jungle, is pressing on the means of subsistence. The uncultivated land is only to be found in the poorest localities, and is used for pasturage, rent-free. When taken up for cultivation it operates in two directions: first, by narrowing the rent-free grazing of the old cultivators; and secondly, by offering a very risky investment for the labour of the most needy.

We pass some thickets of date palms where the date is taken for distillation into "toddy," the favourite spirit of the country.

At the principal stations the native passengers are served with water by a Brahmin, from whom, being of the highest caste, all persons may take without defilement. He goes along the train with his brass vessels; a sudra, or low-caste man, stoops, and in his open hands placed together, and raised to the level of his mouth, receives the precious liquid. The vessel of the Brahmin is not touched, else he would be defiled. A Brahmin asks for water, and is served with it in the smaller vessels, from which he drinks, there being no defilement between Brahmin and Brahmin.

Bellary stands on one of the driest plateaux of the Presidency, and at the termination of railway communication towards the west. It is a very large district, where we were hospitably received by Mr. Huntly Gordon, the collector. An extension through the cotton district of Dharwar by Hoobli to the seaport of Carwar, on the Arabian Sea, is contemplated. This district was heavily visited by famine, the effects of which are still visible. Crowds of people had come into the town to witness a grand religious procession, the animation of which might well have deceived a spectator into the belief that the reported sufferings from famine had been exaggerated. But a visit to some of the country villages dispelled that impression. In one which we examined, there are one hundred families, seventy of whom are landowners, and thirty are landless. When all are mingled together the difference in the condition of the two classes is not readily distinguished. On my request the headman of the village placed all the landed men on one side, and the landless on the other. This at once disclosed two distinct phases of humanity—the comparatively well-to-do landowner, clean and well fed, and the lackland "coolie," thin, eager-eyed, half starved. I questioned these as to their present means of living, which they said were most scant and difficult, as the landholders were straitened by the famine and employed no labour; and the only thing they could do was to gather stalks of corn (large thick reeds from which the ears had been harvested) and carry it in bundles to the town to sell for fuel. What little they got from this was eked out by gathering and eating the seeds of weeds, which had been left to ripen after the regular crop had been removed. Poor creatures, they even take out the rafters of their wretched huts and sell

K

them to buy food. The native officer, an intelligent man, in answer to my question whether this was a typical example of the agricultural villages in the district, said it was a favourable example, as the people here, being within a few miles of the principal town and station, had chances which more remote villages did not possess. There are 2,200 acres of fine land in this village, paying a rent to Government of £70 a year, more than a third of it being Inam, and therefore rent free. The ten largest ryots in ordinary years, and before the late famine, employed thirty labourers all the year; but since the famine they have not been able to do so, and the labourers must shift as they best can. They were on the verge of starvation.

Before commencing the examination of witnesses each day in regard to the famine, we have generally been able to arrange a visit to the country, starting in the early morning to avoid the heat of the sun. A man had that morning been found dead in the streets of starvation, and we had before us a landholder of 30 acres who had been found selling the rafters of his house to buy bread for his children. He told us his story, which was simply this—that he had been so much reduced by the famine that he had first sold one of his bullocks, then the cart, and finally was selling the roof of his house to get the means of buying food. He had borrowed a bullock and cart, and he and his wife had come 20 miles with his load, to raise 5s. to tide over a little longer, in the hope that they might live to pick their cotton crop two months hence! We raised a little purse for them, and it is impossible to imagine the thankfulness of the poor souls thus rescued from starvation.

Mr. Lewis, a missionary who has been thirteen years in this district, says that the small landholders, paying £1 each to Government, are a sober, quiet, well-conducted people, who in their way work hard. Before he came here he lived in Somerset and Devon, and comparing the condition of the people here, in good years, with that of the agricultural labourers of these counties, he thinks them more free from care and better fed, not so well lodged, but having less expense for clothes and education. Eating, gossiping, and sleeping are the happiness of their lives. Their religion, in his opinion, is a custom, and though very impressible they are very conservative of old customs. No man beyond the age of eighteen to twenty-four, or woman from fourteen to fifteen, is unmarried. Mr. Lewis finds a ready hearing among them, and is careful not to offend them by criticism of their objects of worship, while trying to teach them a purer religion by repeating a parable of our Lord, and speaking simply to them upon the lesson it unfolds.

The railway station here is fortified, and there is a fort, on a rocky hill like Edinburgh Castle, within which all Europeans could take shelter in case of need. The place is garrisoned by two regiments and a battery of artillery, being in the close neighbourhood of the Nizam's dominions. There are fine roads in all directions; and, for the English, once a week, polo and the band, and most nights an entertainment of some kind.

The black soil very much resembles the prairies of Illinois. It is cultivated carelessly, much at present lying uncropped for want of means, and that which is cropped very foul with weeds. The cotton crop, which is generally grown by advances from Bombay merchants, is short, but thick and regular, and tolerably good when fairly cleaned between the rows.

CHAPTER X.

HYDERABAD.—NIZAM'S COUNTRY.

THE country continues much the same till we cross the Toongabudra river, when we enter the territory of the Nizam. In the doab between this river and the Kistna the land is good and well cultivated, and the flocks more numerous. That portion through which the railway passes north of the Kistna is thinly peopled and much of it waste. The native rulers seem to recognise the propriety of not encouraging population on poor land. In the few villages one sees the people seem to be in a more prosperous state, their houses and temples more substantial than those on our side of the border.

At Shahabad we leave the main line and travel 120 miles by the Nizam's railway to Hyderabad, passing through rather a poorer country, interspersed with granite boulders and rocky hills, some crowned with hill forts. The Nizam is still in his minority, and the country was governed by Sir Salar Jung and a co-regent. The total revenue is a little over three millions sterling from a population of nine millions, and an area of 80,000 square miles. Within five miles of the capital we maintain a large European force of infantry, cavalry, and artillery, and a native force, the two including the "subsidiary force," paid for, under the Treaty of 1800, by the revenue of the "ceded districts;" and a "contingent" force which, by the Treaty of 1863, is paid for out of the revenue of the "assigned districts" of Berar. The combined force is at the disposal of the British Government for preserving the internal tranquillity of the Nizam's dominions, and for the purpose of a general defensive alliance. The ceded districts passed at the time entirely into the hands of the British; the surplus revenue of the assigned districts of Berar, after payment of the "contingent," is handed over to the Nizam. This arrangement will continue as long as the contingent is maintained, the assigned districts being held in trust for that object. Berar is the richest part of the territory of Hyderabad, and is managed by British officials under the Resident, Sir Richard Meade, who is also Commissioner of Berar, and has been forty years in India, and only six months home during that long period of service. The Residency is in the vicinity of the city of Hyderabad, and is a fine house in a great park, with all the officials of the mission lodged in houses within its walls. It contains also quarters for a regiment of soldiers as guard.

The eastern side of the country, comprising one-third of the Nizam's territory, is irrigated by tanks, and produces rice abundantly, and the people live on rice. It yields two crops in the year, and pays a high rate of assessment to the Government, much higher than in any part of British India, and the people are generally prosperous. On the west side, which comprises two-thirds of the territory, the land is dry and comparatively poor, and the people live on grain. In Berar, where the finest quality of black cotton soil prevails, the people did well during the time of high prices of cotton from 1862 to

1867. Since the fall in price, at the end of the civil war in America, they turned to oil seeds, which they now grow largely for export at Bombay. The ryots have lately received a thirty years' settlement, under which they may sell or let their land, or any portion of it. But any tenant who had not acquired "occupancy right" before the settlement cannot now do so.

In former times it was the custom in this State to give large tracts of country to high officers during their lives; but this was always subject to withdrawal at death, and the son did not succeed unless a new grant from the sovereign was issued. It was found that the cultivator is more secure of justice under a direct holding from the sovereign through his officers, and the country is now all so held, with the exception of some large hereditary estates. Subdivision is not prohibited, and when carried too far may become a serious evil, but in the opinion of both the co-Regents, separately expressed to me, there is no remedy for it. There is one great distinction between our mode of assessment and theirs. They assess in proportion to the value of the crops cultivated, taking most largely from the more valuable crops of the richer land.

A very promising coal-field, interstratified with iron, has been opened in the eastern part of the country. Specimens of both were shown to me by the engineer, who said that the iron had been pronounced, on examination by Dr. Stenhouse, to be equal to the best Swedish. A railway, 220 miles in length, has been proposed and surveyed to open up the country, which would connect the capital with the navigable waters of the Godavery, and tap this coal-field at two-thirds of the distance, and afford an outlet for it at both ends. The nearest coal-field to Hyderabad by railway at present is 940 miles. The proposed line would open a coal supply within 150. But immense though this advantage would be to the Nizam, it would be still more important to us. Both the Bombay and Madras Presidencies at present draw their chief supply from England.

A paper showing the great value of cheaper coal in India was issued by the Public Works Department in 1876. It shows how the working of coal in Bengal has provided employment, that its influence is felt as far as the Punjab and Rajpootana, and that by its use abundant crops are distributed, and cheap transport of surplus produce to the sea-board effected. "The development of Indian coal-fields, and the cheap distribution of coal, is," in the opinion of the Public Works Department of India, "one of the most important questions pressing on the attention of the Government, and no efforts should be spared to attain this object." Here is a favourable opportunity which the Nizam is anxious to adopt. He prefers to do so without incurring further obligation to the Indian Government, but, from some jealousy, is denied the privilege of raising the necessary capital in London on his own credit. One would have supposed that the Government of India, with its hands full of uncompleted works within its own territory, would have been eager to encourage an enterprise involving neither responsibility nor obligation, and which could not fail to be advantageous to the interests of the people of both States. The difficulty has now, 1883, been got over, and this railway is under construction.

The city of Hyderabad is, in point of population, the fourth city in India, about 400,000. We rode through it on elephants, as the people were not very friendly to strangers, many of them going about with swords in their arms, and pistols in their belts. The streets in the afternoon were full of people, buying and selling, dressed in every variety of colour, and with much more liberality of clothing than is common in the lower country; for the city is nearly 2,000 feet above sea level. We extended our ride to a tank or lake which supplies the city with water, the wall of which is formed by arches of masonry laid on their sides, the arches pressing against the water. Here, entering a steam launch, we navigated the lake among its picturesque bays and granite islets, closing the day, in January, with what would be thought a beautiful summer evening in England.

The Nizam in no instance, during the late famine, paid for relief work in grain, always in money, and there was no difficulty in purchasing grain. The normal condition of the ryot is to be in debt. It is the same in Persia, where the whole cultivation is dependent on irrigation. The people are all in debt, and every penny is exacted by the Government that can be squeezed out of them. But they have abundance of food, and are strong and hardy. The Hindu too often spends all he gets, and will not make provision for a future that must therefore take care of itself.

The revenue of the Nizam, with the alienated lands, and the surplus from Berar, is upwards of £3,000,000, one-tenth of which was remitted during the famine. Berar is the richest part of the Hyderabad territory. It is at present administered by the English Commissioner; but will probably be returned to the Nizam when the young prince reaches his majority. The price of a sheep in Hyderabad was then 3s.; of a milk goat, 6s.; rice 1d. per lb.; wheat, ¾d.; millet, ½d. Most of the nobles and upper class are as unlearned as the English of the same class were in the fifteenth century, while the people are said to be superstitious, bigoted, and unscrupulous.

I breakfasted with Sir Salar Jung, who took me through his palace and stables. He had some famous Arab blood in his stud, which was also otherwise good. Among his numerous reception rooms was a suite prepared specially for the Prince of Wales, who was, however, unable to visit Hyderabad when in India. I had also an interview with the co-Regent, who is a member of the reigning family, a very civil old gentleman, with a gold belt, and a blaze of diamonds at its buckle. In all his experience there had been only one such famine in the land as that of 1877–8. Subdivision of their land by the cultivators might certainly proceed too far, but in the opinion of the co-Regent there was no remedy. "It is the custom of the people to subdivide among the sons of the family, and who can interfere with that?"

CHAPTER XI.

AHMEDNUGGUR.—POONAH.—BOMBAY.

We again entered the Bombay Presidency at Sholapore on the 9th of February. It is a considerable place, with a population of 53,000, and the seat of a cotton factory on the joint-stock principle, with a capital of £80,000, and employing 600 people. The factory is fitted with the newest machinery from Manchester, and has been established two years. The only drawback to its success is the price of coal, which is six times higher than in England. The hours of labour are not restricted, generally eleven daily, the people working every day, and resting each alternate Sunday. They manufacture from Indian cotton, grown in this and neighbouring districts, the coarser goods suited to the Indian market. The wages in comparison with Lancashire are as nearly as possible in the proportion of one month's work here for one week there. The Lancashire machinist who superintends the working says that under such circumstances Manchester cannot compete with them in Indian goods. Young men, women, and children, seem all very deft at the work, and every part of it appears to be conducted much as the same work is at home. It will be a great matter if this business proves financially successful, as there is no class which our rule has pressed harder upon than the native weaver and artisan.

On the morning of the 10th we drove to Ekrook Tank, a work planned by Colonel Fyfe, and opened in 1871. It is calculated to irrigate for the whole year upwards of 15,000 acres, and commands nearly 18,000. As yet only one-tenth of this takes the water. The advantages of its application, when combined with ample manuring, are most satisfactorily shown on the land of a sowcar, or native banker, who manures his land with a mixture of night soil and street sweepings, at the rate of forty tons an acre, which he buys at 1s. 6d. a ton in the town, and carts it. The land is planted with sugar-cane, kept under constant irrigation, and the produce which I saw being reaped, squeezed and boiled, yields sugar worth £30 an acre, at a cost of £5 for the manure, £1 for the water, and 10s. for the land —which leaves a large margin for labour and profit. Comparing this with the management of the indolent cultivator, who takes everything he can out of the land at the least cost of labour, and with no attempt to improve or maintain its fertility, it may be doubted whether the system of dandling and protecting him is good either for the country or himself. The law of this Presidency now makes him a ward under the collector if he gets into difficulties; and the collector, already overwhelmed with work, instead of allowing him to be legally sold up when his means and credit are gone, may interpose and try to make a profit for him out of the land from which he could draw no profit himself! As this may be the position of thousands at the same time, the notion that the collector can do this successfully seems absurd.

On the black soil when the rains set in, the land becomes so sticky that wheel conveyance, except on hard roads, is nearly impracticable. During famine, even though the roads or grounds be practicable, there may be no oxen to be got. This happened at Kaludgi, sixty miles from this station, where 5,000 men left the public works, and themselves carried corn as a speculation, buying it from the merchants at the railway, and selling it successfully at Kaludgi for their own profit. This was successfully carried on for some time when no other transport could be obtained.

We arrived at Ahmednuggur on the morning of the 12th of February, after being on the railway all the night. As the morning broke we were passing over a new line made during the famine, which gives a shorter route to Calcutta, and thus obviates the descent and ascent of the Ghats. The country is bare, and not much of it cultivated, except the rich black soil in the hollows. The rivers Beema and Seema traverse the country, which is sparsely inhabited (116 to the square mile), and there are vast tracts of uncultivated land. We are now in the Deccan, the country of the marauding Mahrattas in Sir Arthur Wellesley's time, and of their descendants, the not over-quiet cultivators, whose alleged oppression by their bankers recently led to violence and bloodshed. This city was captured by Sir Arthur in 1803, and the memory of the officers who fell at the breach is kept green on a monument on the old wall near the gate, on which are the names of Major McKenzie and Captain Grant of the Ross-shire Highlanders, and Captain Plenderleath of the Native Infantry.

During the day we were engaged in taking evidence, and towards evening we traversed the city, examining the samples of corn exhibited in the market, where I found the price of wheat nearly as high as ours, this year, at home. The natives everywhere were most civil, the collector, Mr. Stewart, and the judge, now Sir William Wedderburn, being both much respected. I was invited by the municipality to open their new water-works, which gave me an opportunity of complimenting them on this most useful improvement, and on the generally happy appearance of the townspeople who thronged the streets.

Comparing the system here with that adopted by the Dutch in Java, which Sir William had visited, there was general prosperity in that island. The secret of this lay in the Dutch having recognised all that was good in the native management. The people have thus been taken along with the Government in everything, and both prosper together. But here the financial state of the cultivators may be judged of by the following proportion of solvent and indebted landowners in a single talook. Out of 970 only 139 are in full possession of their land; of 725 the whole produce goes to the sowcar, and in the case of 106 their land is uncropped for want of means. The Government assessment is blamed for this state of affairs, but the following figures seem to show that if the people paid no rent for the land, their position would be little affected. In ten cases in which the crops were sold by auction the average price realised was twenty times the amount of the Government demand. The Hindu law of Menu lays down the right of the State, in time of peace, as one-sixth the produce of good dry land. It is not, indeed, a question of rent, but of the crushing advantage which the law gives the creditor over the cultivator. The land of a native chief in this neighbourhood was lately settled at a rate 125 per cent. higher than the Government land, and the people were quite satisfied, because the sowcar's power is restricted. The answers to a series of questions put to the general body of sowcars here state that the interest they charge varies with the credit of the borrower. Where sufficient security is lodged money may be profitably lent at six per cent. per annum. But the rates required from the cultivators are 12, 24, and 36 per cent., according to the security. Out of 100 rupees borrowed, 50 per cent. is for expenses of cultivation, 15 for marriages, and 35 for household expenses. In the last ten years the profits made by the money-lenders have been more than absorbed by their losses. The civil courts are declared by all parties to be very expensive and dilatory, the costs amounting to 25 per cent. of the claim, comprising ten per cent. for stamps, eight for vakils or pleaders, and seven for miscellaneous expenses. The proportion for stamps is excessive, and is believed to yield a large revenue to the Government beyond paying all the expense of the courts. Out of one hundred decrees not more than twenty are executed. Many years' saleable produce, they say, would not liquidate the total amount of the village debt, and the sowcars would willingly compromise for half. They allege that during the famine they supported 50 per cent. of the ryots.

The cause of these financial difficulties may be traced to several sources. There has been a collapse from the temporary prosperity produced by the high prices of cotton during the war in the American cotton States. This has been followed by seasons of scarcity and drought upon a class of soil which, being naturally retentive of moisture, has not demanded the same arrangements for artificial irrigation as have been provided in other parts of India. The people themselves are less continuously industrious, and their exhaustive system of husbandry, with, at the same time, an increasing and home-staying population, must, with each new generation, leave a smaller proportion for each individual. The general body of the community is thus becoming poorer, and their dependence on the chance of seasons greater. All this diminishes the value of the security which the cultivator has to offer to his banker, who, in his turn, finds it necessary to demand a higher rate of interest.

The subject is one of vital importance, and will receive further elucidation as we proceed.

Five-sixths of the cultivators here are embarrassed by debt, the total amount of which is estimated as equal to seven and a half years' rental of their land. The Government take from them 130,000 rupees as rent, and the sowcars 240,000 as interest, reckoned at an average rate of 24 per cent. About 700,000 acres in this district are lying uncultivated from want of means and of bullocks to plough. Good black soil is let at 1s. 9d. an acre, a rate at which money might easily be made if the cultivators had any capital. Wells are everywhere preferred to canal irrigation on equal terms of cost.

There is a Government farm at Kandeish under the management of Mr. Stormont, 1,100 acres in extent, 500 of which are under the plough, and 100 in experimental plantations. One-third of the cultivated area is deep black soil. The chief points aimed at are the production and distribution of better and cleaner seed to the cultivator, experiments on the effect of manures, introduction of improved implements and of new plants, and the improvement of native breeds of cattle by crossing with indigenous and European animals. There are two leading kinds of Indian wheat grown here—yellow, of very good quality, weighing 64 lbs. a bushel, and with irrigation and manure yielding 18 bushels an acre; and white wheat, weighing 58 lbs., which is better suited to dry cultivation. Irrigation on black soil, without manure, Mr. Stormont considers injurious. An intelligent native farmer will not irrigate this soil more than once in three years, that being its turn for manure. The native plough goes deeper than the English with the same power applied, and it is better suited to the land and the working cattle, and to the means of the cultivator. As all begin to sow the land on the same day, when the village priest gives the signal, a joint share in improved implements will not work. The most promising branch of this experimental farm is that which enables the manager to distribute, to the headmen of villages, bulls of an improved breed. Of the new trees, the *Cæsalpinia coriaria,* which produces pods yielding tannin, is being rapidly spread, and the *Inga dulcis,* which grows rapidly for hedges, is useful for ploughs and fuel, and is capable of being coppiced. Near the sea-coast the carob tree, which in the Mediterranean islands and coasts is so productive of cattle food, is being tried. The natives of Kandeish are clever agriculturists, but have no capital, and depend on the sowcar. The labourers on the experimental farm are so well employed that they will not work much more than half time, as they can earn fourpence-halfpenny by a short day's work, and that suffices them.

I visited the American mission schools here, with Dr. Fairbank the head of the mission, where the children are taught in their own language; and also a normal school for the preparation of native teachers; and had an interview with an American clergyman and his wife, the latter of whom conducts a woman's mission of native women converts, or children of converts, who visit the women of the city and villages, and find a ready welcome. The converts are chiefly among the lower castes, but the mission is glad to get the poor and lowly, for whom few care, but who with their children are educated, and so become really superior to the castes who formerly looked down upon them. I had a long conversation with these good American people, modest, but earnest and self-reliant, carrying on a noble work with little to cheer them beyond the consciousness of good and faithful service. Other missions here are also active. An English orphanage has been opened, where 200 orphans from the famine are being tenderly cared for and educated.

We arrived at Poona on the 14th of February. It is a charming city, 2,000 feet above sea-level, the resort of the principal officials of the Presidency of Bombay from July to October, during the rains. The weather in the intervals is then delicious, the air cool and the sky cloudless. This lasts for two or three days at a time, then down come torrents of rain which lay the dust and cool the air, and cover the land with verdure. There is a large army corps of all branches stationed here, to which is added, during the season, the Governor and his staff and council. A river flows by the city, and the public gardens on its banks, with the military bands, are the place of evening resort. There is a drive under an avenue of fine mango trees, which form a complete over-arching shade, and alongside of it a "lady's mile." The houses of Europeans are numerous and handsome. The city itself has a population of 120,000.

Within a few miles there is a mountain range to which picnics are made, one pretty point being Lake Fyfe, a vast artificial reservoir, which, besides supplying water to the city and suburbs, and the cantonments and powder mills, is capable of irrigating 100,000 acres. Its effect on the market gardens within a radius of some miles around the city is shown by the most luxuriant crops of every kind, outside of which the country at this season is barren. The canal is carried for sixty-four miles, and gradually for all that distance along the flat, in which the railway also runs, its refreshing and vivifying influences are spreading with an annual increase. The bund or embankment, placed at the gap through which the outfall of the hills passes, is a wall of masonry, a mile long and a hundred feet high, an engineering work which is highly creditable to the skill of its constructor, Colonel Fyfe.

We are now in the capital of the Deccan, in a dry region where the crops often fail, and whence in former times, prompted perhaps by necessity, the Mahrattas, after reaping their own scanty harvests in November, used to start out on predatory expeditions all over Southern India to plunder the more industrious races of the plains, returning in the spring to spend the fruits of their rapine at their leisure. Our rule has put an end to this with a strong hand, but without substituting so easy a method of remedying the natural poverty of their position. Hence arise periodical distress and a large measure of discontent, manifesting itself of late years in violent attacks on the money-lenders, and in bands of robbers—dacoits—quite capable of wider extension if favourable circumstances should occur. The European officers are kept in a state of uneasy suspicion, watched by a society of natives who act as the people's protectors, the publicity of whose proceedings, through their discussions and newspapers, is really a safeguard to the Government.

There are two hundred members of this society, the leader of which was examined by us. He stated that the society had been chosen by 20,000 landholders, to state their views to the Commission, and among that number were included Deccan and Treaty sirdars of large property, as well as small landholders and labourers; so that all classes interested in land in the Deccan were represented. He is a pleader in the courts, a very sharp, intelligent old man, who, so long as he kept to the subject he thoroughly understood, was most interesting and instructive. He strongly advocated the native Punchayet Courts, and showed that, if they were substituted for small cause courts, five-sixths of the business of the civil courts would disappear. He argued that suits respecting land should go to the civil courts; all others to Punchayets. For such cases no long scientific process of investigation is required. One-sixth only of the present litigation would remain for the superior courts, in which alone pleaders would appear—the parties stating their own cases, at a minimum of cost, in the Punchayets. The number of cases for the whole Presidency appears great, but, when divided among the 22,500 villages in it, would give but six or seven cases for each. The Punchayets should not be, however, in every village, where personal interest might be evoked, but at central stations. Both sowcar and ryot would prefer the Punchayet, which should have the power of obtaining the attendance of witnesses.

The well-meant attempt to restrain the accumulation of interest, which was introduced in 1860, by fixing a limitation of three years to current accounts, had, he said, greatly increased litigation, and had proved injurious to the borrower, in consequence of the necessity imposed on the lender to renew the bond, which thereby led to the introduction of compound interest. For the creditor, to prevent his claim being barred by time, not in order to recover the debt, must file a suit every third year, the cost of which thus falls on the debtor four times in twelve years instead of once. The bond at each time is renewed with added interest. The debt thus assumes four new forms during a period of twelve years, and, with interest at 33 per cent., doubles itself every third year. Five pounds borrowed thus, with compound interest, in twelve years become eighty, if no part of the principal has been paid. Under the old system the same sum, at simple interest, would in twelve years be only twenty-five. The ruinous effects of this must be obvious. Nor does it end here, for the costs of the decree are each time added. Crores of rupees are thus thrown away in the civil courts, inimical feelings between parties are increased, and documents are fabricated to the ruin of each other. It is believed that hardly a man goes to a court and returns without some falsehood. The judges under such circumstances find it difficult to administer justice, and the litigants, occupied in legal disputes, neglect their farms. The consequence had been an enormous increase of litigation, the suits filed in Bombay, in 1860, having risen from 91,000 to quite double that number annually since that time. There was no complaint from the ryot or the country to lead to this legislation, from which all parties were most desirous to revert to the former twelve years' period, with the safeguard of a pass-book to be provided and filled up by the money-lender, and kept by the borrower, without proof of which having been done any action at law should fail. The charges under the new Stamp Act were much complained of, the smallest cases paying in proportion more than great ones, and the largest share of this revenue being thus taken from the most necessitous class. If, as is generally believed, the revenue exacted for court fees yields a large surplus to the State after paying all the expenses of the judiciary establishment, no time should be lost in removing this just cause of complaint.

A native landowner who holds inam, or rent-free, land, with nearly 200 tenants, told us that the rent paid to him was about one-sixth of the gross produce. His people hold from three to twelve acres each, on an annual lease, under which he admitted they may be turned out, or have their rent raised, as he may find possible and convenient. But he and his society claim that Government should grant a thirty years' lease, and limit its demand to one-sixth of the surplus after deducting all expenses of cultivation.

Great dissatisfaction was expressed at the absence of any results from the Deccan Riots Commission, especially in regard to the Limitation Act. The report, they said, had dispelled the charge that the people were suffering as a consequence of their own extravagance. The poverty is undoubted. Seventy-five per cent. of the cultivators, on the poorer class of land, are hopelessly indebted. A man with twenty acres cannot therefore, in most cases, cultivate over five. Things are tending gradually to abolition of credit, and a change in condition from ryots to labourers. In Dharwar, one-fourth of the land has in this way passed into the hands of money-lenders, non-cultivators, who sublet to tenant-labourers, from whom they exact half the crop, and also the Government assessment. The average amount of this is one shilling an acre, and, as there are ten lacs of outstanding arrears in the Poona division at present, two million acres are in risk of passing from the ryots into the hands of Government. In that case the Government might re-issue this land without conferring right of mortgage, but with permanency of possession so long as the rent was paid. Many officers of experience advocate this course as the one best suited to the natives of India.

There has been a plague of rats all over this part of the country, which have made fearful havoc of the crop, and reduced by two-thirds what would otherwise have been a fair crop. In certain seasons they breed and spread with immense rapidity, and with the return of heavy rain disappear as quickly. Following a year of famine, this has greatly aggravated the sufferings of the Mahratta people, who are the most improvident in India.

The Deccan consists entirely of trap soils, which divide themselves into broad distinctive features; first, the black, which is the best in quality, and is let by the Government at 2s. to 3s. an acre; second, the red, at 2s. to 2s. 6d.; and third, a shallow, grey, dusty, hot, sandy soil, which is charged at 6d. to 9d. an acre. The two best form two-fifths of the whole, the least productive being the most extensive. The deep black soil holds moisture best, and for a long time, and will draw it from the atmosphere, even though rain does not fall. Certain parts of the Deccan are more subject to droughts than others. At the crest of the Ghats there may be a rainfall of 300 inches, and not one-fourth of it ten miles eastward. Droughts come with comparative frequency, but severe famine only once or twice in a century.

The Forest Department is very active in this part of the country, and contemplates dealing with one-seventh of its area, much of which is already heavily timbered. This is three times the proportion of woods to cultivated land in England. They are now enclosing great breadths, on which seeds of all kinds of forest trees, suited to the climate, are sown broadcast during the rains. This enclosure shuts out the people from much of their grazing land, and from getting timber for fuel and other purposes to which they and their fathers had long been accustomed without stint. Great discontent is thereby aroused, which will most likely, in the opinion of the police, lead to crime, and may become a source of danger. To a certain degree, the preservation of forests is most desirable, but their extension by the forest-officers in a reckless manner, and with too high a hand, should be most carefully guarded against.

The all-important subject of improved agriculture was constantly in the mind of the Governor, Sir Richard Temple. He had projected a plan of agricultural education for Western India, which was in course of preparation, and in his hands could not fail to be carried out with effect.

Whilst at Poona we made several excursions into the country, the last being eighteen miles through the tract watered by the canal from Lake Fyfe. There were large breadths of bearded wheat, all in ear on the 19th of February, and showing the promise of an average English crop, shorter in straw but thick on the ground. There was a marked distinction in parts recently manured, which were taller and thicker, as if they had been treated with nitrate of soda. The charge for irrigation is 4s. an acre. Two crops are grown in the year, great millet for the rain crop, and wheat for the winter crop. Manure is applied as often as it can be had. Large eight-bullock ploughs were working on the fallow land in preparation for the rain-crop, grinding down the clods into fine mould. They were moving the soil to a depth of ten inches, managed by two men, one holding the plough, the other guiding the bullocks, which were yoked two and two ahead of each other. The plough is a powerful wooden wedge, shod and pointed with iron, which bores into and rends the hard but friable earth, bursting and breaking it in large lumps, which are partly crumbled by the friction of the wedge, and partly broken into mould by the feet of the cattle. The two men by voice and action urge them to their work, shouting to each by name, either with an endearing epithet or the reverse, as encouragement or intimidation may appear expedient. The cattle were fine large white animals, and pulled very honestly.

Leaving our kind and hospitable friend at Poona, the Commissioner, Mr. Robertson, after an hour and a half we reached the edge of the Ghats, whence we descend 2,000 feet through fine scenery, the mountains rising all round as the railway winds its way by a gradual fall into the low country, through deep-wooded ravines which, in the rains, sparkle with numerous waterfalls amidst the verdure. We push on through Bombay to Guzerat, the day beginning to dawn as we neared Surat, where the country is rich and productive. We cross the Taptee river, here navigable to the sea, and in two hours more we come to the splendid river Nerbudda, of great width, a strong tide running up from the sea. A new railway bridge of iron is being constructed, to rest on tubes of large diameter, as the present bridge was found not sufficiently firm to withstand the rush, and occasional shock, of floating trees in time of flood. Thousands of people were at work, men and women, in hoisting and placing the enormous tubes, and in all the other engineering operations connected with this stupendous work, which is on a scale of magnitude beyond the conception of native rule. The cost is justified by the fact that this line will connect Bombay with Delhi and Northern India, and independently of its own traffic will (or would but for the unfortunate break of gauge) provide a direct outlet to Bombay for the produce of that extensive and fertile region. For many miles we had been passing through the rich black cotton soil of Surat and Broach, the latter city having a fine position on the north branch of the Nerbudda.

At Baroda the country alters; the soil is a reddish loam clothed with splendid trees, which look all the richer after the comparatively naked black soil country. The flag of the Resident's house (where the former Guickwar attempted to poison Colonel Phayre) is seen amidst rich parklike scenery. Near Nariad there is very fine cultivation from wells, tobacco and garden crops beautifully farmed, and every sign of prosperity among the people. Their holdings are separated by low hedges; *every one has his well, and, where this is attainable and the water good, I believe no other irrigation in India can compare with it.* Each man can use it when and how he pleases, and as he must keep bullocks for the labour of his land, and he and his family on these small holdings do most of the work, they hardly feel the cost of lifting the water. Their villages are generally tile-roofed, the people are better clad, and their bullocks are stronger and bigger than I have yet seen. All this is the result of "well" irrigation on a better soil, with a climate seldom so extreme in drought as to cause severe scarcity, never famine. The head men engage with the Government for the rent of the village, and allot to each cultivator his share of the payment.

At Memadabad I visited the court, the Treasury, and the hospital. The work of collecting the revenue is done by the native officials. That morning they had sent off by rail to Bombay 100,000 rupees. An armed guard is kept at the Treasury room. In the hospital there were only two cases—one a poor little boy whose arm had been broken by the stroke of a stick from a ryot, into whose crop the boy had allowed his cow to stray; and the other an elderly man who, on interposing to protect the boy, was brutally attacked by the same fellow with his weeding hook, and desperately wounded and cut. The man had been arrested, and was awaiting trial.

In the early dawn next morning we drove to Kaira, a place of 12,000 inhabitants, along a fine road with sheltering trees. The town stands on the high bank of a river. From the top of the collector's house there is an extensive view over a rich, well-timbered country. There are many monkeys, some very large, and though they injure the crops, no one molests them. This care of life in regard to the lower creation, is a principle of Hindu religion perhaps more strictly observed than that of care of their fellow creatures, outside the circle of their own family connection. Within that circle they are wonderfully kind. Hindus of high caste never take life. Some are strict vegetarians, and in order to preserve life will frighten away fish from parts of a river where they have reason to expect English officers to come in quest of them. Even the much-abused money-lender refuses all advances to fishermen. On one occasion I came upon an extensive enclosed park with shelter sheds, maintained by a native banker, into which horses, no longer fit for use, were charitably received and fed, that they might wear out their lives in quietness. And yet female infanticide is undoubtedly too common, 64 females to 100 males being not an unusual proportion in the population. A native judge explained this to me by the great desire among the lower class to intermarry with the higher, a lower man being ready to pay a needy man of the higher order a large sum of money to induce the son of the higher rank to marry his daughter. But when the lower man has no money, as is too often the case, the female infant is apt to be neglected and allowed to die.

A growing feeling of dissatisfaction with English rule, which I had met with from the same reason in other quarters, found expression in this district. Before the mutiny, and under the old East India Company, the people had learned by experience that our practice was to do away with all the cesses and duties with which native governments formerly harassed their people. But since that time our course has been constantly to add some new tax. They do not acknowledge the advantage of our great civilising works, but they do feel their cost. The needful roads and works which were formerly carried out by the collector and his staff, at moderate cost out of the revenue, are now committed to engineers with expensive departments, and a vastly increased annual outlay. Disaffection is aroused, we are hated by the Mussulmans, and disliked by the Hindus. This is not likely at present to take tangible form, as there is no head under whom the various dissatisfied persons would unite. But a crusade is being preached here against the infidel Government by the Mahommedans, and on all sides there is a readiness to blame it on every occasion. There was lately a tumult at Surat, during which the civil authorities had to take shelter in a public building from the violence of the people, and which might have led to direful results but for the sharp interposition of troops. It is singularly illustrative of our rule that, though the people for six generations have known no other, we are still strangers among them. Our representatives come and go, now faster than ever, and we and they look on each other with distrust.

Ahmedabad, a city of 120,000 people, was formerly the seat of the kings of Guzerat. It is placed on a river in a finely cultivated and beautifully timbered country; the founder Ahmed having left a memorial of his taste in an extremely elegantly proportioned small mosque with two minarets, the stone and marble carving of which vie with the exquisite work at Agra. A neighbouring modern Jine temple, built thirty years ago, somewhat in Hindu fashion, only less ugly, cannot compare with this in beauty.

On this line of railway 1,500 people are employed, of whom little more than fifteen are Europeans. The native guards and other employés are most reliable, sober men. In ten years not one has been dismissed for drunkenness. During the four monsoon months, when traffic of all kinds diminishes on account of the rains, the manager gives a large proportion of the men their leave for that period, to which they make no objection, as their mode of living is simple and cheap, and they have abundance saved to enable them to take a holiday with their relations. Théy return when the rains cease, the railway company being richer by having saved their wages in the idle time, and the men having had their holiday. Englishmen in the same position would have saved nothing, and could not afford a holiday.

On our return we halted at Surat, another ancient city, with a population of 107,000. It stands on the navigable river Taptee, within twelve miles of the sea, and is the earliest seat of our Indian possession. The Dutch preceded us, but we rendered such useful help to the Mohammedan monarch that the Dutch were ousted, and the "Company" put in in their stead. Within the city is an ancient Dutch burying-ground with grand tombs, now crumbling to pieces. Outside the city walls is the English burying-place, where our earliest representatives, who died here, have been buried in tombs of great magnificence. The principal one, or rather one enfolding the other, is in memory of two brothers Oxenden, who more than a hundred and fifty years ago seem in succession to have held the chief posts. There is another to an English captain who commanded "the Mogul's Castle and fleet" in 1658, and many others on a grand scale, indicating the great importance attached to Surat at that time.

This city, seated on its navigable river, in the midst of a rich country, reminded me of the site of Bordeaux on the Garonne. But here the river is silting up, and vessels that formerly came with their cargoes to the quays can come no longer. The roads even in the neighbourhood of the town are very bad, and there is an evidence of decay in the unrepaired ruins of houses, and the slipping and undermining of the river banks and quays. The most substantial of the old works are the broad stone stairs down which the people go to wash their clothes in the river, but these are the work of the old rulers, matters of such everyday usefulness being too seldom thought of by us.

In this neighbourhood a certain village, which claimed to pay not more than 1,000 rupees as its fixed permanent assessment, on the ground of a sunnud of a former ruler who had fixed it at that term for ever, was visited by the collector, who, on inquiry, thought himself entitled to disregard the alleged sunnud, and to put the assessment up to 4,000 rupees. The village appealed to the courts, and a decision was given in its favour, against which the collector appealed to a higher court, and was again defeated. Upon this, Government, being beaten in its contention, passed a resolution that such cases in future should not be tried by the judicial court, but by the revenue officer!

We visited a village of 1,400 acres, the Government rent of which was £280, and the debt due to their bankers by the cultivators £6,000. It is all fine arable land, and yet the cultivator, paying only 4s. an acre, with the sun, the rain, the double crop for next to nothing, is deeply embarrassed. There is something wrong, for the crops were good and the land reasonably well cultivated. It is due partly to the right given to the ryots to mortgage the public land, and partly to the improvidence of the people, who vie with each other in feasts and expenses at deaths and marriages, there being moreover no more common cause of dispute than the right of precedence of their bullocks and themselves at village festivals.

The native judges in the small cause courts, by whom four-fifths of all law cases are decided, guide themselves on the case as placed before them by the pleaders. They do their best to arrive at a fair decision upon the statement before them, but do not think it their duty to take trouble to see that an ignorant or uneducated man has his case all told. Two moonsiffs whom I examined were evidently afraid of the additional trouble which might be thrown upon them if pleaders were not allowed in the small cause courts. But pleaders are distrusted by the ryots, and a clever pleader may get too much of his own way with an easy moonsiff. I see no reason why the moonsiff should not, with the parties before him, examine the case thoroughly, without pleaders, and be held responsible for giving just judgment after careful investigation. The climate and the Indian disposition favour all kinds of easy workmanship, but the immensely higher rate of pay which the moonsiff gets, compared with anything else he could earn, would warrant Government in demanding from him a thorough examination without the help of pleaders, the best of whom are generally secured by the wealthiest litigant.

Continuing our journey southwards, the land is an alluvial plain sparsely inhabited, stretching from the mountains to the sea, seemingly capable of great improvement. Before reaching Bulsar we cross two tidal rivers navigable for small craft, which carry fuel from the jungles to Bombay. At Daman there is a small Portuguese settlement still extant, the principal use of which now is as a refuge for the distressed, fleeing from the law in British territory. The flat country is now rapidly narrowed by the nearer approach of the mountains to the sea, and many "doons" or small rounded hills (odd that they should have the same name in India and at home) stand out of the plain and gradually break it into height and hollow. As we approach Bassein the country narrows more and more, a strip not two miles wide from hill to sea, all the good patches of which are carefully laid into little squares to hold the water on the rice, which is nearly the only crop grown here. Rivers up which a rapid tide is flowing are crossed on bridges of immense length, and the conical hills covered with trees and jungle are very picturesque. Many sailing boats are plying about these creeks and rivers, and stake nets set quite across some of the branches of the stream catch all that comes. Fine tall full-leaved trees and splendid palms clothe the drier grounds which rise above the level of rice cultivation, and small fields of thick sugar-cane are fenced with a close thatch around them against the wild and tame animals which evidently frequent this quarter.

As we cross one of the longest bridges, Bassein rises on the promontory seawards, an ancient Portuguese walled town, now deserted, with churches and streets, the seat of early commerce, taken from them by the Mahrattas two centuries ago, and afterwards by these abandoned. The walls of the town remain, and the spires and towers, but all is roofless, and has been so for more than a hundred years. There is a rich country in its neighbourhood, famous for vegetables and plantains which are daily conveyed by boats to the market at Bombay. The scenery here is lovely, resembling the Kyles of Bute without its rain, with white-sailed trading craft plying up the wide inlet which here separates the island from the mainland. It narrows to a slender stream where road and rail cross it on the outlet to the east.

In a few miles more we reach Bombay, which, take it all in all, is the most picturesque city in India. Viewed from Government House, on the sea-point of Malabar Hill, I have seen nothing finer. Hospitably lodged by the Governor in charming rooms in a bungalow above the battery, I joined him at sunrise on the verandah. It had been blowing hard all night, the wind beating through the open venetians, and waving the wide musquito curtains about my bed. The wind had fallen in the morning to a light breeze, but a long swell was still running up the beach and round the point into the bay. There a large fleet of fishing boats had run for shelter on the previous evening, and now in the first daybreak they were all moving outwards. Across the bay is Colabar Point with the lighthouse, and further landward the fine group of buildings forming the Government offices; still further the city itself, and the masts of the large fleet of ships always lying in the roadstead. Beyond are seen the islands in the inner harbour, backed by the high mountains of most picturesque shape, on which the full fury of the south-west monsoon bursts. Beyond all the sun was rising in a cloudless sky, touching every point with light, and brightening up the white sails of the fishing boats as in slow succession they rounded the point, and breasted the long swell below us. After spending some days on the business of the Commission, including a lengthened examination of the Governor, I bade adieu to Sir Richard Temple, and to India, with a most grateful remembrance of the kind and friendly hospitality which I experienced in every part of it.

CHAPTER XII.

EGYPT.

In the middle of March, 1879, I arrived in Egypt, on my way home from India. Sir Rivers Wilson was then the principal adviser of the Khedive, and he readily afforded me every assistance to examine the agriculture of the country. This I was desirous to do, in order to compare that of India with Egypt. Accompanied by Mr., now Sir Aucland Colvin, who had been some months in the country, and by an Egyptian officer who knew it well, we traversed a considerable portion of the Delta, and afterwards visited the sugar estates of the Khedive, 100 miles above Cairo.

There are five million cultivated acres in Egypt, of which the Khedive and his family, and the Daira, possessed about one-fifth. The Land Revenue was then about £4,000,000, and the country population between five and six millions. There was thus about one person to each cultivated acre, and adding the rental of the private estates of the reigning family, each acre yielded an average of twenty shillings of Land Revenue. India has also one person to each cultivated acre, but each acre on an average yields only two shillings of Land Revenue.

The winter crops on the ground—wheat, barley, beans, and clover—were everywhere fine, and within a month of being ripe. The land was clean and well cultivated, and the cattle were either house-fed, or tethered so as not to tread down and waste the rich green food on the field. Cotton was being planted on land most carefully prepared for it, and in high condition. Steam-pumps were pumping water from the river or canals upon the land, the Nile at this season being low. Wells are used where river or canals are not available.

Beans were the heaviest and finest of the crops on the ground. This crop is largely grown, and, as it requires little water and no manure, it gives a great return. Wheat, a bearded kind, is the most widely-grown cereal, and promised an excellent crop, quite equal to the average of England. Barley was not so good. Clover was particularly fine, and grown everywhere for forage. I saw no land in bare fallow. Manure is collected by carrying in earth to bed the stalls in which the cattle are placed at night, and where they receive forage. Nothing is allowed to run to waste. The manure from pigeon-houses sometimes brings as much as £20 from a single house. The plough is much the same as that used in India, and is drawn by two bullocks.

The cultivators are much stronger in body and limb than those of India. They live very plainly, coarse bread and an onion being their daily food, and cooked beans a luxury. Their villages are more permanent in structure than those in India, but built of the same material, clay, and the walls of the houses plastered, as in India, with cakes of cow-dung, which are being thus dried for the fuel with which they cook their food.

The cotton soils yield the most valuable crop, and are cultivated with the greatest care. They are of two kinds, of which that yielding the brown cotton is the more valuable, both for quality and length of staple. The yield is from 300 to 400 lb. an acre, and the crop is worth from £15 to £20. The white cotton is more productive, but of less value per lb. The characteristic properties which render these soils severally suitable for each variety of cotton are well known.

The cotton is an exhausting crop, and succeeds best when not taken oftener in succession than once in three years. But it has proved so profitable that, on good soils, it is generally taken every second year. Clover is sown with it, which is taken as a forage crop after the cotton is removed, and this may be successfully followed by Indian corn. No manure, other than the deposit of the Nile, is given to the cotton crop, except on the poorer cotton lands, where pigeon-manure is occasionally applied. Good cotton land will fetch 30 to 40 years' purchase of the Government rent. The cotton land is generally so well suited to the crop that it is believed much heavier crops might be got by higher cultivation. A fair crop will yield, besides the 400 lb. of cotton, 800 lb. of cotton seed; and the Egyptian cotton seed cake is said not to require, like the American, to be decorticated, as it is naturally free from a substance which, in the latter, requires this process. This cotton cake is now largely imported into England for the feeding of cattle and sheep.

The cultivator is generally in debt, like the similar class in India, and like him was subjected to very heavy rates of interest. But he holds his two or three acres inscribed in the Government books, and considers it private property, a freehold, subject only to the Government demand or assessment. The Sheik, or head-man of the village, collects the assessment from the landholders of the village, and pays it in one sum to the Government collector. The Sheik and the village accountant keep the accounts, which are open to the inspection of each landholder.

Since the mixed courts, comprising three European and two native judges, had been instituted, the cultivators have their rights fairly secured. But, for the same reason, they are more frequently sold up for debt, as the new court is more prompt in the execution of its judgments. Formerly no sales of the holding took place, a cultivator failing for five years to pay his assessment being ousted by the Government.

It was authoritatively stated in the House of Commons, eighteen months ago, that the extortionate demands for interest to which the landholders had previously been exposed had been superseded by the Crédit Foncier, under which they were provided with funds on reasonable terms, and that great advantage and comparative prosperity had been the result. But the more recent report of Lord Dufferin reveals an existing state of matters quite as bad as I found them in some parts of Egypt in 1879. This, no doubt, had arisen from the late disorganisation of government there, and we must hope that better times are in store for the Egyptian peasants.

About 100 miles up the Nile from Cairo are situated the great sugar estates of the former Khedive. We proceeded there by railway, near to one of the stations of which stands the sugar factory of one of them. The premises are of the most modern plan and construction, and the whole arrangements most complete. At this factory there are two 60-horse-power engines, and an entire set of apparatus for expressing the juice of the sugar-cane, and converting it into fine raw sugar. Tramways are laid from it across the sugar plantations, to carry home the sugar-cane. There are a number of these factories, with similar arrangements, upon this portion of the Khedive's estates, admirably designed and executed, but carried out at an enormous cost, and with works on too large a scale for the produce of the land attached to them.

Where the land is let here for farming it yields a rent of £3 an acre, but it bears three crops in the year, as it is completely supplied with that wonderful renovator, an abundance of Nile water.

Above Cairo the country (which is comparatively a narrow strip bordering the sides of the river and bounded on the outside by a sandy desert) is formed by embankment into vast enclosures, which are enriched by being flooded with Nile water every year, by the river covering them and depositing its mud. But on the wide Delta, below Cairo, the river is carefully enclosed by embankment from overflowing, and is let in or pumped up as required by the growing crops—cotton, maize, wheat, beans, or millet. Here there are two or sometimes three crops in the year. The embankment is kept in order by corvée, or forced labour, contributed in due proportion by the cultivators, whose growing crops may be totally destroyed by a breach in the embankment at the time of "high Nile," though, in such a case, there is some compensation in the larger deposit of mud for the benefit of the following year.

The great fertility of Egypt is due to the rich mud carried down every year by the Nile, and deposited over the surface of the land either by natural overflow or artificial irrigation. There is a wonderful provision of nature in the mode of the annual rising of the river, which derives its waters from two sources. The smallest but earliest supply comes from the melted snow in the mountains of Abyssinia, by the Blue Nile, which first fills up, with cold clear water, the lower part of the bed of the river. This is followed, a few weeks later, by the swollen waters of the White Nile, the mud-bearing and warmer waters from the interior of Africa, which fill up the river, overflowing the land and enriching it. If by any natural convulsion the process were reversed, and the cold clear water came latest, and over the surface of the mud-bearing water, Egypt would soon become a desert.

The great cities of Cairo and Alexandria, which, in addition to that of Egypt proper, derive considerable wealth from the interior of Africa, comprise within themselves one-tenth of the whole population (650,000 out of 6,700,000), and take off from dependence on agriculture a large portion of that labour which in India has little other resource than that of employment on the land. Wages are higher in Egypt, but food is dearer than in most parts of India. The cultivators of the land, the Fellaheen, are none of them in possession of large holdings like the great Zemindars of India. They are more in the condition of the smaller land-holders with permanent rights; few are so low as mere tenants, and none so dependent on others as the Indian labourer who has no land.

Writing in September, 1883, I have good authority for saying that, under the present Khedive, with the guidance of the great knowledge and experience of Sir Evelyn Baring, there is every prospect of an early prosperity in Egypt. The Khedive is honest, brave, and true, and the ablest man among the public men of Egypt. He failed at the outset of his rule because he left everything to his Council. But he is not likely to fall into that error again, for Egyptian Councils require guidance, and he now knows this, and has both the will and the capacity to afford it. The English troops, it is confidently expected, may soon be all withdrawn, as the English commander of the native army has obtained their confidence, and the people are easily ruled when they feel the touch of a just government.

CHAPTER XIII.

INDIAN FAMINES AND THEIR LESSONS.

INDIAN famines are caused by drought, sometimes aggravated by war or other pressure, and their severity may be measured by the scarcity and high price of food-grain, and the consequent mortality among the people affected. The greatest sufferers are the landless class, who live by wages, and the village artisans, who are dependent on employment by the cultivator. The remedies adopted will appear from the measures heretofore taken by Government and private persons, and the cost incurred by the State. As the records previous to the present century are imperfect, I confine myself to a short review of the greater famines since 1800, and will endeavour to elicit the lessons which they afford.

In 1803 and 1804 there was partial famine in Bombay, Hyderabad, Northern Madras, and in the North-West Provinces. In Bombay the effects of the scarcity were aggravated by war. The price of grain was four times its usual amount. The deaths do not appear to have been recorded. Grain was imported into Bombay by Government, and exportation was prohibited. Public works and hospitals were opened for the strangers who sought aid in the towns of Bombay and Surat. In the North-West Provinces, Government made large remissions of revenue, gave loans to the landowners, and offered a bounty on imports. In this case there was active Government interposition. But the whole expenditure could not have replaced one-twentieth of the crop that was lost.

In 1813 there was a famine in Guzerat and Rajputana, and the adjacent portion of the North-West Provinces. Grain rose to six times its ordinary price. The distress was great, three-fourths of the cattle in Rajputana died, "man ate man," skeletons lay in every direction, and when rain came many died of fever, brought on by low condition. The Government of Bombay refused to interfere either with export or import, declaring that unassisted trade, if left to itself, could do more to relieve distress, and effect an equable distribution of supply, than Government could with all its resources. It was not stated that any food was imported, although 325,000 tons must have been lost.

In 1833 there was a terrible famine in the northern districts of Madras. The price of grain, however, seldom rose higher than three times its ordinary amount. Out of a population of 500,000 in Gantur, one of the districts affected, 200,000 are said to have died of famine. Government, having been taken by surprise, did very little to relieve distress, the whole expenditure not having exceeded £30,000, which could not have replaced the hundredth part of the food that was lost.

In 1837 the North-Western Provinces experienced a most extensive and severe famine. Grain rose to three times its ordinary price. Probably a million people died of famine. Government interposed early and with earnest effort, but on the principle that their duty was limited to finding employment for those who could work, and leaving the infirm and helpless to the charitable public. To this some aid was given by Government, but not as a matter of right. Remission and suspension of revenue were freely given to the land-owners, amounting to nearly half the land revenue of the affected country. Loans and advances were given only for land improvement or seed-grain, as it was considered loans for other purposes led the people to rely too little on themselves. Less than one per cent. were relieved on works, or gratuitously. The suffering endured left a wide-spread and lasting recollection of the horrors of the famine. The loss of food-grain may be estimated at 1,200,000 tons. The total expenditure on relief, if all laid out on food, would have replaced but 118,000 tons. In this famine the population severely affected was fifteen millions. Of these one-fourth may be assumed to be of the landless class, to whom no Government aid by remission or loans was given. One-half of these, we may suppose, were able to support themselves by the Government employment offered to those capable of working. The other half would be the helpless and infirm who were left to the charitable public, and among these, in all probability, were the one million famine deaths, for the prevention of which the Government on principle refused to make any provision.

The next considerable famine was that of 1861, again in the North-West Provinces and the Punjab. The population affected was thirteen millions, and food-grain rose to three times its ordinary price. The area of distress was fortunately surrounded by countries with good crops, into which it is believed half a million of the poorer class fled for support. This, and the supply that could thence be conveniently drawn, greatly mitigated the pressure. The same policy was pursued by Government of providing employment for those who could work, and leaving the helpless to the charitable public. But both plans were carried out in a more provident and thorough manner. Large relief works of permanent utility were opened under supervision of professional officers, and an ingenious test was contrived for the weak who could not travel for work far from their homes, and for those who obtained gratuitous relief. This was by giving them cooked instead of raw food (the cooking being prejudicial to caste, and intensely disliked by the people), with the further test of serving it only to those who submitted to residence in an enclosed poor-house. Less than one per cent. of the population received employment and relief. Notwithstanding the advantage of good crops in the surrounding districts, 200,000 people died of famine. The quantity of grain estimated to be lost by the drought was 1,210,000 tons, and the total quantity imported to make good that loss 180,000 tons.

The next severe famine was in 1866–7, which spread from the east coast of Madras upwards, being most severe on the coast of Ganjam, and afterwards to Orissa, and finally extended to Behar and Northern Bengal. The price of grain rose to five and six times its average amount in Ganjam, six times in Orissa (where, indeed, for a time there was none to be had at any price), and three times in Behar. The famine deaths in Madras Presidency were 450,000. The number employed on relief works was 12,000. Gratuitous relief was given to 31,000 persons daily—mainly in the form of cooked food (after the example of the alleged success of this plan in 1861), and in relief-houses or camps, managed as in the previous famine in the North-West Provinces. The total number relieved was but one-third of one per cent. of the population.

In Orissa no one appears to have observed the approach of famine till it was upon them. The winter rice crop on which the country mainly depends was almost totally lost. There were no sufficient food stores; and yet, as no apprehension was entertained either by Government or people, there was no rise of price to tempt imports, or to check consumption. In May,

1866, it was suddenly discovered that no food could be bought in the market for the gaol prisoners and Government establishments. By that time the southern monsoon rendered importation impossible. The South could afford no relief, Ganjam being equally distressed. By the end of November 10,000 tons of food were with great difficulty got into the country, and given away to the starving people, but meantime one-third of them had died. The drought was followed by great floods which drowned the crops in the low country, so that in 1867 the work of relief had to be taken up again. The total amount spent by Government was £1,270,000. The famine deaths were over 1,000,000.

In Behar and Northern Bengal the famine on this occasion was not so severe. Relief works were opened and gratuitous distribution of food was made, both affording relief for four months to less than one per cent. of the people; but the whole expenditure having been only £23,000, the Government can claim little credit for their efforts to preserve life, the famine deaths having been 135,000. Landholders, under the permanent settlement, generally ignored their responsibility for the poor, and the urgent need of a Poor Law to enforce this duty where that settlement is established was clearly exemplified. All the money spent by Government in the famine of 1866–7 would not have replaced one-twelfth of the food-crop that was lost.

The great famine of 1868-9 included a large portion of Western and North-Western India. It was most severe in Marwar, Bihanor, and Ajmere, but included the other native States of Rajputana, and Central India as far as Jhansi, also Hissar in the Punjab; and with less virulence large tracts in the Central Provinces, the western half of the North-Western Provinces, the south and east of the Punjab and Guzerat, and North Deccan in Bombay. The population affected was about forty-five millions, seventeen of which severely. The famine deaths were over 1,600,000, and the Government expenditure £720,000, which would not have replaced more than the twentieth part of the food-grain that was lost in the British Provinces alone. One million, two-thirds of the population, emigrated from Marwar. Little was done in the native States to help the people. But, in the British, the coming difficulty had been early foreseen, and for the first time the principle was declared that Government held itself responsible that no preventible deaths should occur. As usual the landless class suffered most. Grain rose to four times its usual price. In the native State of Rampur, money was distributed to the necessitous with success by the headmen of villages.

With the famine of 1868–9 closes the economical system which up to that time prevailed. The famine in Behar in 1873–4 was met with a promptitude and energy heretofore unexampled. Sir George Campbell, the Lieutenant-Governor of Bengal, had acted as a member of the Commission which had investigated the circumstances of the unhappy famine in Orissa in 1866. He was therefore fully alive to the great importance of early as well as adequate preparation. And the Viceroy, Lord Northbrook, was fresh from and imbued with the English feeling that this country deemed itself responsible that there should be no recurrence of the horrors of that time. On Sir George Campbell's retirement, from impaired health, his successor, Sir Richard Temple, entered with characteristic energy upon the immediate direction of the famine campaign. The inquiries they instituted led them to estimate the deficiency to be provided at not less than 480,000 tons of rice. Every probable or even possible contingency was provided for. Food-grain rose between three and four times above its ordinary price. Government entered into direct contract for its importation from Burmah, and a vast machinery of transport was improvised to convey these supplies into the various parts of the country in good time, by which an average of upwards of 3,000 tons a day were laid down in the district in the three and a half months from March to June. Notwithstanding this active interposition of the Government, private trade continued fairly active.

Having thus provided the necessary food, there was neither need for, nor desire to impose with the old severity, the test which in former famines had effectually repelled multitudes from seeking relief. Work was offered to all who chose to accept it, but without much expectation that it would be of after-value to the State, and uncooked food or money was given at their homes to the helpless and infirm. Instead of tests which imposed a laborious walk of twenty or thirty miles upon emaciated people, or cooked food which offended their most sacred feelings, the personal knowledge of the relieving officers was held to be sufficient proof of need. The result was that, inclusive of the small landowners to whom advances in grain were made, three and three-quarters per cent. of the population were thus maintained gratuitously for six months, and a little over four per cent. on works for nine months. Had the famine continued for a whole year, the surplus grain, which was afterwards sold at a great loss, would have been all required. The cost, which was unprecedented in amount, was thus considerably increased, but the result was also without precedent, in that there were no famine deaths, nor the fatal epidemics which accompany and follow emaciated condition, nor even that pauperised character which is so commonly anticipated as a consequence of gratuitous relief. Costly as it appears when compared with the previous famines of this century, the expenditure in Behar is not more, when spread over the average eleven years in which famines occur, than one-fourteenth of the annual expenditure on the poor of the United Kingdom.

This brings us to the great famine of 1876–8, the most wide-spread and the most costly in life and money since the beginning of the century. It extended over more than half the Madras Presidency, the whole of Mysore, the Deccan district of Hyderabad, and Bombay. It thus embraced a population of fifty millions, but also reaching later the North-West Provinces, Cashmere, and part of the Punjab. The continuance of excessive pressure was longer than in the famines of 1874 or 1868. Food-grain rose to three or four times its ordinary price.

The treatment of this great famine was not uniform. In Bombay, when the monsoon rains failed in 1876, the Government were ready with plans of large public works, which they placed under the control of professional engineers, declaring that relief should not be made attractive, but so arranging that all who chose to work should be secured a bare subsistence. The numbers employed on these works for thirteen months were 285,000, or less than three per cent. of the population of the district affected. The number gratuitously relieved daily for the same time was but one-third of one per cent., and even this extremely minute assistance was burdened by the test of coming to relief camps to procure it, only the bedridden or incapable being relieved at their homes. The total expenditure by the Government was £1,140,000, and the famine deaths are believed to have exceeded one million. Many of the landless class were left in a state of great poverty and emaciation, a too easy prey to epidemic fever.

In Mysore the loss of crop was reckoned at two thirds of an ordinary harvest over the whole Province, thus causing a deficiency in the usual food supply of 540,000 tons. If the whole money expended on relief works, and otherwise, had been employed in the purchase of food it would not have replaced more than one-eighth of the deficiency. The confusion that arose, in the vain effort to meet such a position by public works and local works, and by gratuitous supplies of cooked food, with or without condition of residence, led to great mortality, and to a complete change of plan after the visit of the Viceroy. No importations, however, were made by the Government. £700,000 were spent in trying to make one pound of food do the work of three, and one million, or one-fifth of the people, died.

The Government of Madras in one respect acted differently. The loss of crop in the most severely affected districts was probably not less than that of Mysore, and if we assume that one-third was saved, the deficiency would amount to at least 2,350,000 tons. Without consulting the Government of India, Madras, on its own responsibility, purchased 30,000 tons of rice, to be stored in very distressed localities, to be ready in case local trade should fail. This was disapproved of by the Central Government, and any repetition of it was forbidden. This rebuff at the outset had doubtless some effect in restraining early independent action. In other respects the want of good understanding between the public works officers and the district officials was much the same as in Mysore, and too much work was thrown upon the latter without adequate guidance from any prompt central authority. Difficulties arose, expenses increased, and Sir Richard Temple was delegated by the Government of India to visit the Presidency. A system of village relief was introduced, by which, on the certificate of the headmen, money was doled out. This was not attended with success, having probably been too suddenly improvised, and with imperfect supervision, for frauds occurred, persons not in need intercepting what was intended for those most in want. In many cases, too, the supervising officers were unacquainted with the language of the people, and incapable of understanding them. As soon as rain came hope returned, and the relief works were quickly deserted. But the mortality had been frightful, two millions having died. Daily relief was given for twenty-two months to an average number (787,000), representing 4½ per cent. of the population affected, which of itself ought not to have cost more than £3,000,000. But the total expenditure is estimated at £8,000,000, so that vast sums must have been wasted in the unmanageable struggle with despairing multitudes who had left their village organisation for employment or relief. The total quantity of food imported into the Presidency was sufficient only to feed nine millions for twelve months, while the famine lasted for twenty-two months.

The scarcity in the Punjab in 1878 was chiefly due to the high prices caused by the export of wheat to England, and the emigration of people fleeing from famine in Cashmere.

In the North-West Provinces the drought of 1877-8 was more severe than in either 1860 or 1868; it spread over a larger area, and the loss it caused was more than double the loss in either of the two former cases. The crops reaped amounted to but one-sixth of an average over the whole Province; thus involving a loss which has been estimated at 3,420,000 tons. The money expended on relief, £200,000, if it had been all laid out in the purchase of grain, would have replaced only the odd 20,000 tons of the above enormous loss. The average number relieved daily for twelve months was 69,450, which is barely one-fourth of one per cent. of the population. Arrangements were made for opening remunerative works, both large and small, and for a time considerable numbers were employed. But a fall of rain was followed by a reduction of the price of food, and by re-opening the ordinary sources of employment. The necessities of the people thus appearing less, greater strictness in giving relief was enforced, and the wage reduced to a bare subsistence. The works became nearly deserted in the beginning of December, but the rain which then fell put an end to the need of artificial irrigation and stopped all field employment. The rain was accompanied by intense cold, which told heavily on the poorer classes, who had been living on reduced rations, and had in many cases sold the thatch of their houses to buy food. The winter crop was promising, but the monsoon of 1878 held off, and the Government had a large scheme of useful works prepared of various classes sufficient for the employment of 9½ per cent. of the population. But these remedies were not found necessary, as rain came in July, and was followed by an active demand for labour, which enabled the Government to close its relief works in October. The famine deaths were 1,250,000, small pox, fever, and bowel diseases having completed what emaciation began. The quantity of food introduced into the country was wholly inadequate to meet the great deficiency of the season.

In reviewing the famines of this century we are at once struck with the meagre assistance afforded by the Government previous to 1874. The only instance of Government relief having been given to an extent exceeding one per cent. of the population severely affected, was Orissa, where the circumstances were quite exceptional. Relief to the extent of one-third of one per cent., less than one per cent., and in some cases nothing, such was the amount of aid with which the several Governments of the country met the inroads of famine. The total expenditure averages but 4d. a head of the famine-stricken populations. It was practically nothing as compared with the loss of food. The prices of grain rose generally three to four-fold. The whole Government outlay, if it had been spent in the purchase of food, would not have replaced the thirtieth part of that which was lost. Various principles of treatment were tried, with much the same result. In one case the Government did nothing; in another they were surprised, and did little; in another they encouraged import and prohibited export. In 1837 they laid down a rule to help the capable, and leave the incapable to charity; in 1861 this principle was adhered to, with the addition of a distance test, and a cooked food test administered in relief houses. In 1866 the cooked food test was partially abandoned, on account of the intense caste repulsion felt to it. The leading desire in affording relief was to make it so unattractive as to repel all but the most necessitous, and to force those who, from age or incapacity, were unable to work, to resort to relief houses or camps for their dole of food. Estimating the deaths in the earlier years, where they are not recorded at the same proportion as those in which they are set forth, fully six millions must have perished of famine.

With the famine of 1874 in Behar a new system was inaugurated. It is the first which shows successful management as measured by the saving of life, for there were no famine deaths. Its characteristics were that nearly eight per cent. of the population severely affected received relief, during its continuance, by the active and early intervention of the Government, and that no one in need of relief was repelled from work, or aid, by distance or other tests. And it was marked by the successful introduction for the first time of the system of village relief and inspection, and by that means the distribution of food to all the really necessitous. A further reason may be added in explanation of its success that this famine was under the immediate control of the Viceroy and his very able Lieutenant, and that there was no superior authority in India to interfere or to be consulted. The expenditure was on a scale up to that time unprecedented, largely increased by the necessity of improvising costly means of transport, and by a considerable loss sustained in a surplus stock of grain food provided, but most of all by the determination that no one should, if possible, die for lack of food. When compared with the annual expense of maintaining the poor in England, the cost of a famine such as this, which comes but nine times in a century, is extremely moderate. As measured by the price of grain, and the apprehensions entertained in the early months of the famine, there can be no doubt of its intensity at that time, and that if the usual measures had been adopted it would have formed no exception to the usual famine mortality.

The lesson of 1874 was, unfortunately, only partially followed in Bombay and Madras in the famine of 1877–8. There was an expenditure on as great a scale, but the preparations were not made with the same completeness or promptitude, and the old system of making relief repellant and unattractive was reverted to. Thousands in consequence died rather than leave their homes, and tens of thousands died on their way to, and in, the relief camps. The system of village inspection and relief, for the first time established in 1874 with so much success, was almost set aside, though this was the remedy which, of all others, proved the most complete at that time. Wherever it was followed in 1877–8 there was comparative freedom from mortality. In so far as it was incompletely followed there was great mortality. Before the end of 1876, one-fourth of the people had begun to eke out their scanty supply of food by resorting to unusual articles which predisposed them to disease. In July, 1877, in Bellary, it was rare to find man or woman in effective condition for labour. Fatal injury to the functions of assimilation had thus arisen before the people were brought within schemes of public relief, the most truly economical application of which, in famine times, is in such early help as will give assurance of life. When the village is deserted, and the family is scattered, depression of vitality comes on, there is no longer desire for life. It is not obstinacy that prevents persons in this condition from seeking relief, but mental depression, which should be dealt with humanely, and not by making relief repellant and unattractive. The greater mortality, distress, and expense incurred in Madras, apart from the main fact of the greater extent and intensity of famine, and the confusion and waste which arose, may, in some degree, be attributed to the unwieldy size of the districts, and the comparatively small number of European officers.

The management of the drought of 1877, in the North-West Provinces, is an exception from that of Behar in 1874, of a different kind. Though the scarcity of 1877–8 has been clearly shown to have been much more severe than either of the two which preceded it, no attempt was made by Government to replace any part of the stupendous loss of food occasioned by the drought. A moderate spring harvest was accepted as having removed the fear of famine. The lessons of 1874 were altogether ignored. The village relief system was not attempted, and the old plan of distance and other tests to render relief works unattractive and repellant were adopted. Careful plans for large works of a public and valuable character were prepared, but were not opened. The people seem to have lost heart enough to face the natural and artificial difficulties with which they were beset, and 1,250,000 of them died of famine. If no value is placed on human life, this famine may claim to have been one of the most cheaply managed in history. It cost the Government but 2¼d. a head of the population severely affected!

In all Indian famines the uniform experience has been that the people at once return to their usual avocations on the arrival of rain, in whatever form relief has been administered. In no instance does it appear that they have been pauperised by gratuitous help in time of famine.

From this review the only conclusion we can arrive at is that the general principles of famine management which proved so entirely successful in 1874 should be the leading guide of the Government in future famines.

The agricultural population of India, which comprises nine-tenths of the people, dwell in villages not holding the land in common, but organised under natural or selected leaders, who are recognised, and in many cases salaried, by Government. Three-fourths of the people are landholders; the remainder are artisans, weavers, and labourers. They have fixed positions in the society, are orderly and considerate of each other, and charitable and helpful to the poor of their community in seasons when there is abundance, or even only a sufficiency of food. If drought and famine come the land cannot be cultivated, the landless class have no employment and no stores of food, and, with want staring them in the face, they break away from their families and villages in search of food.

When families are broken up, and all the ties of order and village organisation are lost, and the poorer people become a moving multitude wandering from their homes in despair, no expenditure, however extravagant, can prevent famine death. It is only by maintaining the village society that order can be completely preserved, and the aid and influence of the natural heads of the people be effectively utilised by the Government. There has been a mistaken desire to obtain some economical return for the food given to the people to sustain life, partly in order to reimburse the State, and partly to prevent pauperising the recipients. The first consideration, however, must be the preservation of life; the second, and subordinate one, the most economical mode of accomplishing this. The medical and other evidence in regard to the first is wholly in favour of the maintenance of the village system as the only effective means of saving life by preserving order, and securing to the people the shelter and little comforts of home which so materially help to economise food. As a rule the Indian agricultural labourers do little hard work between seed-time and harvest. It is very important that they should be at hand to take advantage of the first reappearance of rain to resume agricultural operations, and there are many ways in which, without much exertion, they can advantageously eke out a moderate allowance of food by little earnings from their richer neighbours. If maintained in this orderly and natural manner, without hard labour being exacted, they would be physically in better condition at the end of a famine year, and would be in a more fit state to resume their usual agricultural avocations, than if fully and more expensively fed on distant labour relief works. The stronger men of the village might be employed with great economy and advantage in carrying food to the villages from the relief centres, and in no other way could their labour be more profitably utilised.

If it be granted that this is the most effective mode of saving life, let us farther test it on the question of greatest economy. It will be admitted that a man on hard labour, exposed to the weather, and away from the shelter, comfort, and convenience of home, will require one-fourth more food than the man from whom no labour is exacted, who must be content, like his betters the landholders, in time of famine to live on short allowance, and who enjoys home advantages. On every four millions expended there would thus be a saving of one million, and on every four thousand tons of food transported a saving of the transport of one thousand, a matter of extreme importance in those parts of the country unprovided with railways and of difficult access. On the same principle it would follow that in a famine-stricken population five millions would be kept alive where no labour is exacted on the same food as would be required for four millions working under a labour test. In other words, one million lives might be saved by giving up that ineffective labour which is admitted on all hands to have little economical value.

But there would be more than this saved. The disruption of Society caused by relief works, and the improvised machinery of superintendents new to the work and frequently ignorant of the language of the people; the necessary neglect of their ordinary duties by the civil officers thus employed; the necessity of maintaining a constant and costly staff of the Department of Public Works, with plans always ready for execution, which, if really beneficial, should not wait for a period in which their execution must be on the most expensive scale; the great public cost of all this would be saved. Further, there would be the limitation by one-fourth of the severe pressure on other districts of India by the necessity of drawing away from them a portion of their ordinary supply of food. When to all these considerations fair and adequate weight is given, I feel no doubt that in time of severe famine, even in point of economy, the saving of food, by exacting no labour, will bear a favourable comparison with the profitable results of the costly labour of famine relief works. The annual sum set aside for famine relief is indeed very moderate for so large a population. Compared with England it is not more than one fiftieth per head of our annual expenditure in the relief of the poor.

This was the main principle of the successful treatment of famine in 1874, and I, with confidence, recommend that it be more fully developed, and more completely carried out in future Indian famines.

The village system would then become the central point and basis of future Indian famine relief. The natural leaders of the community, the headmen, who are now the *quasi* officers of Government, who know the individual circumstances of the people, and have the deepest interest in their welfare, should be more fully recognised, and their position made so desirable that their active co-operation might be insured; and especially would this be desirable in localities difficult of access, if it should hereafter be deemed proper to buy and store food, under their supervision, for the landless class, in years of abundance. In cases where relief is given by Government gratuitously, the repayment of some proportion of the cost might be imposed on the village property as its reasonable share of the burden, and, at the same time, as a check on over liberality with the public money.

CHAPTER XIV.

THE FUTURE.—CONCLUSION.

The future success of British rule in India must depend on the Government adapting itself to the progress of knowledge amongst the people, for the handful of white men who now administer it must more and more rely on the intelligent assistance of the most capable men among the millions whom they govern. These are comprised in the proportion of 20 millions living in towns of 5,000 and upwards, and 200 millions distributed over the country in villages with an average of 400 people in each, who, as cultivators, labourers, and artisans, are directly dependent on the land. It is thus a vast assemblage of peasant cultivators and their dependents, who under our rule are rapidly increasing in numbers, and pressing on the means of subsistence. If the population continues to increase at the same rate as during the last ten years, even though, as in the preceding decade, it should suffer a heavy loss by famine and its consequences, there will be 15,000,000 more people to be fed in 1891 than in 1881. This is the great problem to be met by the Government and people of India. It can be successfully encountered by a very moderate increase of crop on each acre of the land now cultivated, and by a gradual and moderate annual reclamation of good land now uncultivated.

The greatest help that can be given towards this object is the early construction of railways in all the richer and more populous parts of the country which are still without them. The most thinly-peopled regions may be left to the last, as they are naturally the least fertile, and in time of famine will be fed without difficulty from the richer countries, when these have railways by which they can export their surplus crop. In the next ten years the present mileage of railways in India should be at least doubled, and even then India would not have one-fortieth of the mileage compared with the population, and area under crop, which is at present possessed by the United States.

The experience already gained in India shows clearly that railways through the best districts may become a very lucrative investment, and Government may find it advisable to keep clear of all complications by reserving in their own power both the choice of locality, and the raising of capital for construction. The State is quite as capable of contracting for the execution of the works as a company, and can borrow the capital for construction on more favourable terms. The Under-Secretary of State said recently, in his Budget speech, that, if the railways already made in India had been started with money at 3½ per cent., the profit to the Government would now be over two millions yearly. It is still in their power to secure this with what remains to be done in the construction of lines in the fertile districts, which as they are opened will, by affording access to markets, vastly increase the motive for improved cultivation, and give new opportunity for that variety of employment which is so much needed in India.

The money already spent on irrigation is considerable, and it has been very profitable where used in repairing and enlarging the ancient river-fed canal system of Southern India. There the water carries an enriching though not plentiful deposit, while the cost of reinstating an ancient work is comparatively small, and the capital therefore moderate upon which the profit is to be realised. But where the works are all new the capital spent in construction is very considerable. And, in those irrigation canals which are fed from the melted snows of the Himalayas, the water comes down at a temperature much below that of the land to which it is applied, and carries with it a deposit which is a barren sand. Most of this fortunately sinks to the bottom of the canal, and thus is in great part prevented from injuring the land. But the effect of this pure cold water on vegetation is only permanently useful when the land is sufficiently manured, and becomes positively hurtful when lavishly applied year after year to unmanured land. Irrigation from wells on each man's land is not open to this objection, as the water is used with economy, and only upon manured land. Any capital of the State hereafter applied for irrigation should be used with careful consideration of the circumstances now referred to.

In the most fertile and best watered land, with convenient access, there is prosperity, and great readiness shown by cultivators to make the most of their position. The price of land there is very high compared with the assessment, and the ryots are fully capable of defending their rights. They quickly accommodate their agriculture to the production of the most lucrative crop, whether it be sugar, jute, tobacco, or wheat, where the soil and climate are suitable. The ryot, indeed, becomes master of the position, and, under the law, he knows how to unite with his fellows and maintain his own rights. Here any change from a money assessment to payment of kind would not be listened to by him.

It is quite different in the poorer land which has no certain command of water. Here it is a struggle for life, with a sufficient supply of the plainest food in good years, and the greatest difficulty and hardest living to get on in seasons of scarcity. Nominally the Government assessment is paid in money, but really it is paid by the ryot in kind, but without any of the advantages of that principle, for he is so deeply indebted that he hands over all his crop to his banker, who pays the Government assessment in money, doles out seed and food to the cultivator, and keeps the rest to repay himself principal and interest of loans which are never other than open. In such regions the cultivator does not attempt to pay off debt. He has no intention to be dishonest, but it is the fact that money advanced on loan to persons in that condition in India can only be repaid out of the crop upon which the advance has been made, by the grain crop when reaped being transferred to the banker, who keeps it all except what is needed for the seed of the new crop, and the maintenance of the people and working stock, till another crop is ready. The cultivators under this system become practically his bondmen.

The principle of payment of rent in kind is the best suited to small landholders in countries liable to periodical visitations of famine. When there is no crop there is no rent due, and this applies equally to loss of crop by drought, or when the land is left fallow. Thus there is no pressure on the cultivator to continue the cropping of land which has become exhausted, and such land can be left, without cost to him, to recruit its qualities by rest. But we have introduced a system, based on English custom and law, which is not in harmony with native views. In the native States the rent may appear higher than in the British, but the ryot pays only for the land he cultivates, and nothing for that which is preparing itself, by rest in fallow, for future cultivation. There is not, then, the same necessity for the ryot to apply to the banker for an advance to meet the Government demand, nor is there good security for a loan where the land cannot be sold for debt. The native banker does not, therefore, find his business so profitable in native States as in British.

It would now be difficult, though in some parts of

the country desirable, to return to a system of produce rents. But in the experiments about to be made of Government Agricultural Banks, we should be careful not to increase the ryot's temptation to incur debt. If his present debts are paid by a composition with his creditors, the money being advanced to the creditor by a State bank, the Government on paying that composition would become virtually the owner of the land. Whatever debt the ryot subsequently contracted would be on his own credit, as he would have no power to pledge the Government land until he had repaid the loan; and in the process of doing so he would have acquired habits of economy and thrift, by which he might, in the course of time, redeem and make it freehold. In the dry countries of India the native system of land tenure, if administered with the same justice as under British rule, is much more conducive to the prosperity of small landholders than ours. If we had maintained the native principle, that the land could not be sold for debt, there would have been less credit given, and the cultivator would have had to rely on his own industry instead of being propped up by borrowed capital. When reduced to poverty he has neither the means nor the motive to bestow labour on improvements. And there can be no escape from the gradual exhaustion of the soil that must ensue under such circumstances.

To the reader of this book abundant evidence from all the drier parts of India has been afforded that the strict application of the principles of English law, as between debtor and creditor, is becoming very disastrous. The Limitation and Stamp Acts, which came into operation in 1861, were intended to protect the debtor against his wily creditor by enforcing short accounts, and to curb the spirit of litigation by imposing a tax upon suits. But, though the revenue has been benefited by the tax, it is at the cost of the poorest class of cultivators, who, being in nearly all cases the losers in an appeal to the courts, have to pay it in addition to their debt. Litigation has at the same time greatly increased by the necessity of an appeal to the courts every third year, instead of once in twelve. The general effect of a well-meant change has thus been ruinous in some parts of the country, but especially in the Deccan, where it has been found necessary to supersede the law by a remedy of a most drastic character.

The growing danger of India, in addition to the rapid increase of population, is the poverty of two-thirds of its landholders, and their consequent inability to check the gradual exhaustion of its soil. Population cannot indeed long increase beyond the means of subsistence, but the pressure on these means incites to their increase by prompting a resort to new land, or by forcing a larger return from that at present cultivated. I believe it to be possible to obtain such a gradual increase of production in India as would meet the present rate of increase of population for a considerable time. One bushel of increase per acre gained gradually in a period of ten years, in addition to a moderate reclamation of cultivable land, would meet the demand of the present growth of population. Considering the generally fertile nature of the soil, and that in most parts of India two crops can be got in the year, this would seem a very possible result. By these two methods, wisely combined, the increase of population may be safely provided for during several generations. The attainment of this will be vastly increased by committing to each Province the direction and responsibility of the operations necessary for its own success, and of enlisting the active assistance of the most capable native officials, municipalities, and landowners in the work. The public debt of India, apart from the reproductive capital spent on railways, irrigation, and other public works, is not more than a single year's income, and nearly one-half of that is obtained otherwise than by a tax on the people, and chiefly by the rent of the public land. These are solid advantages, which should afford great encouragement in the arduous task of governing India. But economy alone in the public expenditure will not suffice without increased production. Every facility towards that end must be given. The people are familiarised with modern resources and inventions. The steam engine, the railway, the telegraph, are accepted and understood by them. They have among them in every Province men of science, of philosophy, of benevolence, and patriotism, and also men who in competitive examinations in this country have held a leading place. And the time has come when the prosperity of India, under our rule, can only be maintained by honestly carrying out the Queen's proclamation of 1858, whereby it was promised that her subjects, of whatever race or creed, should be freely and impartially admitted to all offices in the service of India, the duties of which they might be qualified by their education, ability, and integrity to discharge.

APPENDIX.

In closing the subject, it may be well to insert here an extract from a letter addressed by me to the Viceroy in February, 1879, before leaving India, which embodies the views most strongly impressed on my mind when fresh from the examination of the country.

"As to the agriculture of India, on the good land where there is a command of water, the cultivators have not much to learn. The most paying crops, beautifully cultivated, follow each other in rapid succession. Their implements are of the most primitive kind, but that they answer their purpose the clean, garden-like appearance of the land sufficiently attests. The rapidity, too, with which the most paying crops are introduced is shown by the rapid spread of the jute and sugar-cane. No one plants the latter without having the land in the finest condition, both of tillage and manure. The crop is often worth fifty years' purchase of the Government assessment of the land on which it grows. Land of this quality when it comes into the market is most eagerly sought after, and fetches almost any price.

"But in the rest of the country, comprising nearly four-fifths of the cultivated land, the state of agriculture is nothing but a system of living from hand to mouth. Three-fourths of the cultivators have no capital. In a good year they have enough for their simple wants; in a year of abundance their banker has something to apply in reduction of their debt; in an unfavourable year they live very poorly, and partly by help of their credit; in a year of famine that is withdrawn, and they have no means left of employing labour, and the poorest of them and their labourers are equally destitute.

"If we had it in our power to begin again, I would revert to the old plan of the Government taking its rent in a share of the produce. That share should bear a relation to the quality of the soil and its situation. On the best soils this plan might have the objection that it would discourage good cultivation when the cultivator did not keep all the increase to himself, and there it might be proper to modify the principle. But on most of the land of India the cultivator puts no capital into the land. He has no cash. His theory is to let the land rest when it has been over-cropped, and to begin again on the land which has had rest. This he used to do till increasing population pressed on the area of cultivation, and obliged him to confine himself within narrower bounds than his fathers—so narrow that he can now spare none for fallow. The land thus has no rest, and is becoming by every round of crops slightly less productive.

"But this would have been different if his assessment had been taken in kind. Then he would have retained land enough to permit part of it to lie fallow. For, as he would be called on for only a share of the crop, he would lose nothing by leaving part of his land idle.

"This payment in money has also made him the slave of the money-lender. Government must be paid to the day, and as the Bunyia is the only capitalist within his reach, he hands over all his crop to the Bunyia as a security for cash advances, instead of paying the Government its share of the produce in kind. That the Government could now, much more easily than in former times, take the rent in produce, there can be no doubt, and means might be adopted to prevent peculation. There would be no occasion for future re-settlement. Having fixed the proportion (for which in India there is much information in the Survey Department), the Government share would rise or fall in value with prices. If it should be determined at any future time to sell the Government interest in the land, it would be found to bear a just relation to its value, which it does not at present. This would really be a grand reform if it could now be accomplished. By releasing the Ryot from the money-lender, it would shut up a large proportion of the Civil Court business, and leave some capital gradually to accumulate in the Ryot's hands, and so enable him to improve his system of agriculture, and to maintain the condition of his land.

"There are two points on which I fear I may differ from your Excellency in regard to famine relief: the distance test, and the confidence Government seems to repose in trade as an effective and economical agent in the supply of food. Our evidence goes to show that the weaker part of the population can, individually, be most cheaply supplied at their homes, and that their condition there is comparatively happy. It may cost more in money, but that will be because more lives will be preserved. Every needless exertion imposed during famine must cause waste of substance, and thus imperil life.

"As to trade, it would be an interference with trade to forbid the export of corn from a famine district, and would most likely prevent any being sent into it. That I should entirely oppose. But I can see little difference in Government making contracts for the commissariat of its army, and adopting the most sure and economical means, by contract or otherwise, for the supply of food to its famishing people, when a calamity more serious even than war befalls them. The Government should pledge itself to nothing, but be prepared to act as circumstances might indicate.

"There are but two ways of meeting famine, as the Duke of Wellington said in 1805. Firstly, by making the more fortunate parts of the country supply the wants of the rest, and the superfluity of one year make good the deficiency of another. Secondly, by rendering as much of the country as is liable to famine-drought safe by an extension of irrigation. But that needs money, and to get money the finances must be in good condition.

"I should venture, therefore, to say, husband the resources of the country by every practicable means, till a safe surplus is accumulated, completing at present only such works as are absolutely necessary. It is a mistake to go faster with irrigation works than the people are prepared to take advantage of. Let useful works be ready for the able-bodied in a famine year.

"I have tried to estimate the cost of a famine. Science tells us, and experience confirms it, that in India you may count on nine famines in a century. The proportion of the people affected reduces the average annual loss to a sum which I bring out wonderfully near Sir John Strachey's annual famine fund—£1,500,000. When we compare this with the annual cost of the relief of the poor in England, which is equal to 6s. 3d. per head of the whole population, it is not more than one-fiftieth of our expenditure when spread over the whole population of India. So that even if there was nothing got back in the shape of relief work, the annual charge would be no heavy strain on the resources of India when her financial equilibrium is restored."

THE END.

Cassell & Company, Limited, Belle Sauvage Works, London, E.C.